To Melanie.
With love

ℓ x

D0852578

THE PRACTICAL ENCYCLOPEDIA OF

PAINT RECIPES
PAINT EFFECTS
& SPECIAL FINISHES

THE PRACTICAL ENCYCLOPEDIA OF
PAINT RECIPES
PAINT EFFECTS
& SPECIAL FINISHES

The ultimate source book for creating beautiful,
easy-to-achieve interiors

Sacha Cohen

HERMES
HOUSE

This edition published by Hermes House
an imprint of
Anness Publishing Limited
Hermes House
88-89 Blackfriars Road
London SE1 8HA

A CIP catalogue record for this book is available from the British Library

Publisher: Joanna Lorenz
Senior Editor: Toria Leitch
Contributing Editor: Geraldine Christy
Designer: Isobel Gillan
Photography: Lucinda Symons (projects),
Rodney Forte (techniques) and John Freeman
(equipment and techniques)
Stylist: Diana Civil
Production Controller: Don Campaniello

Printed and bound in China

© Anness Publishing Limited 1999 2001
Updated © 2002
3 5 7 9 10 8 6 4

CONTENTS

INTRODUCTION

Recent years have seen a surge in interest in decorative paint effects. Perhaps as technology plays an increasing role in our lives we are eager to counteract its seeming impersonality by creating our own style and expressing our individuality more clearly in our homes.

This book aims to help you explore a wide variety of techniques for making a decorative impact on your own interior. There are inspirational effects, from simple colour treatments for the walls to fantasy decoration for furniture and accessories. All are described in easy-to-follow steps and there are project ideas for themes to follow or adapt as you wish.

ABOVE: An ordinary box is transformed with a dark wood effect. The black fern effect is painted freehand.

OPPOSITE: This Roman fresco of the 1st century AD from the House of Livia, Rome, features a dark green wall painted with garlands of flowers.

THE DECORATIVE USE OF PAINTING

People have used paint to decorate the walls of their homes since the time of the Stone Age cave dwellers. These early hunters used simple earth pigments to adorn their caves with huge scenes of wild animals.

By the time of the early civilizations wall decoration was becoming more sophisticated and reflected the great advances that mankind had made. The ancient Egyptians painted the walls of their temples and tombs with scenes of everyday life, and decorated furniture and architectural detail. They used a range of pigments that included a wondrous, brilliant blue made by crushing the mineral stone lapis lazuli.

In the Minoan Palace of Knossos on the Mediterranean island of Crete, amazing frescoes have been found that date from around 1600 BC. These are startling in their apparent modernity. Many of them feature the plant and marine life that is found in and around the island, yet they are painted in such a stylized fashion that they seem almost like abstract shapes. Mycenaean pottery that dates from about the same time also displays stylized naturalistic forms with banding and stripes.

A thousand years later on mainland Greece the great temple of the Parthenon was decorated with a profusion of bright colour, which seems strange to us today when we view the white marble of the building sparkling in the sun on top of the Acropolis in Athens. Greek pottery featured painted and engraved decoration, with geometric borders that are still regularly used. Designs such as the Greek key pattern immediately convey a classic look to any item or area they decorate.

It was the Romans who invented what we now know as mural painting. With the frontiers of their empire ever widening they were able to obtain many new pigments and increase the colour range of their paints.

BELOW: This cave painting of bison from Altamira in Spain dates from Palaeolithic times.

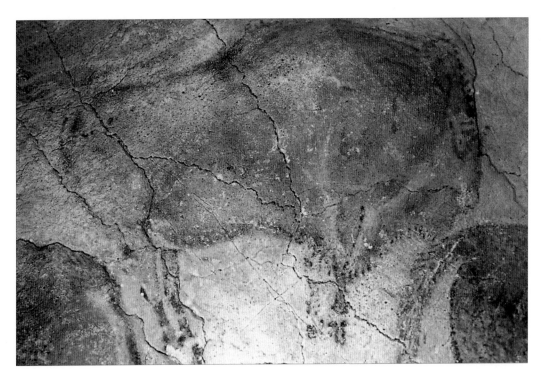

ABOVE: *The Throne Room of the Minoan Palace of Knossos, Crete, dates from the 16th century BC. The decoration here shows a fresco of a griffin and plants. It is painted with red earth pigments and a double white stripe borders the room.*

The city of Pompeii lay covered and protected under the volcanic ash of Mount Vesuvius for hundreds of years, yet many of the colours are still as bright as when they were first painted. These houses of the 1st century AD are painted with frescoes that depict full-scale modelled lifelike figures and a wide variety of activities and subject matter from mythology to eating and drinking. The decorations were used to display the social status and wealth of their owners and the Romans enhanced their villas with clever creativity. They became masters of faux effects, extending and manipulating space in interiors by painting realistic architectural detail with marbling and graining and painted entire *trompe-l'oeil* settings.

The tradition of fresco painting came to the fore some hundreds of years later in the religious painting of the Renaissance when artists revived the classical rules and attitudes of the ancient Greeks and Romans. In terms of the decoration of interiors, supreme art and

craft came together in the work of Leonardo da Vinci and Michelangelo. Leonardo's *Last Supper* in the convent of Sta Maria delle Grazie in Milan is a monumental wall painting within a false room that stretches back into the landscape, while Michelangelo's frescoes on the ceiling of the Sistine Chapel in Rome are among the greatest works of Western art.

At about this time the nature of paints also began to develop, and oil-based binders led to new possibilities for artists and craftsmen. Oil-based paints took longer to dry and gave the opportunity for further experimentation. Artists used oil paints to create free-standing paintings, and the art of fresco wall painting was abandoned. In the meantime technical ability developed and it became essential for artists to be able to imitate surfaces and fabric textures accurately in paint and to render perspective correctly. The trade routes to the East were a source of new colours and pigments.

Trompe-l'oeil ceiling decoration continued right through the 18th century, and with the revival of neoclassicism in architecture new paint effects were used for walls. Proportions became important and rooms were divided by panels and ornamental details. Travel became easier and more popular in Europe and colours and ideas were gathered and exchanged. Faux effects were used for marbling columns and for decorating furniture and small items with expensive woods and tortoiseshell in an effort to display the appearance of wealth. Layers of thinned paint were used on top of each other as glazes to achieve depth of colour.

Aniline dyes were invented in the 19th century. This meant that new, vibrant pigments that were not as costly as natural earth resources could be used. The art of paint effects became within everyday financial reach, though they were still executed by specialist craftsmen. Public buildings such as public houses and theatres were decorated in a grand style that we associate with the Victorians, with wood graining, marble effects, ornamented patterning and gilding.

By the 1930s and the arrival of the Art Deco style, paint effects had become simpler. Combed and textured techniques were more prominent and a limited, though specific, colour palette was used. In the following decades paint effects were used only by specialist craftsmen as wallpaper and, later, flat surfaces became the fashion. Matt, soft sheen and gloss paints meant that light could be played with in a simple way in keeping with the modern feel for space.

Meanwhile, parallel with the efforts of the well-to-do to appear even more grand by copying rich and expensive materials, country people were using their own paints in effects and designs that were individual to their own cultures. This simple and easy-to-live-with look has much character and appeal to today's technological age. The use of natural paints and their soft colours allows the creation of a comfortable home rather than one that is painted to reflect status.

In Eastern Europe and Scandinavia bright colours were used, probably as a foil against the cold, white winters, with simple painted patterns that became traditional and were passed down through the generations. In the United States the pioneering spirit of the early settlers led to the development of freehand designs that were influenced by the many countries from which they had originated, producing a style of their own. They used milk paints in muted colours to decorate walls and furniture and simple storage items, such as wooden boxes, were painted in flowing naturalistic designs both for protection and decoration.

OPPOSITE: *This 16th-century fresco from the Villa Barbaro in Maser, Italy shows a* trompe-l'oeil *garden scene.*

Texture, too, was an intrinsic part of decoration for many country people. In France, for example, the craft of pargeting was used. This is a method of decoration in which a design is incised into wet plaster. Many effects can be produced in this way, from all-over geometric designs to randomly placed motifs.

The current interest in traditional folk decoration runs hand in hand with a respect for natural materials. Thus wood graining, marbling and other special effects such as gilding have been revived for new and exciting uses. As we try to recapture our past, effects such as distressing and ageing, and the look of antique materials such as bronze and copper with verdigris, have become fashionable.

Many new paints are available to today's decorators. No longer do we need to rely on local resources. The invention of synthetic paints means that we can choose to paint with any colour we desire. We also have a massive choice of finishes for different effects and numerous paints for various surfaces. There are special quick-drying formula paints that allow us to achieve a new decoration for a room in a matter of hours. Painting equipment, too, has improved, with softer paintbrushes and new solvents that make cleaning up easy. There are specialist brushes for specific techniques and to help you reach into any niche or corner.

Paint is now one of the easiest ways to transform your home, allowing you complete freedom in choosing any style you wish with a multitude of colours and textures. You can choose to recreate a historic period from the past or let your imagination create a futuristic setting quite unlike anything anyone has yet seen. Ranges of traditional paints are being revived from every era and location so you can decorate authentically if desired. Manufacturers produce a constant stream of new paints, such as interference paints, metallic finishes and pearlescent effects.

Many people now enjoy refurbishing junk furniture into new items through simple paint techniques. This is an inexpensive way to add even more style to your home. Car boot and garage sales, junk shops and flea markets are an amazing source of items that have been thrown away as useless. In most cases it is easy to make a few easy repairs and paint the piece to give it new life at a fraction of the cost of a new item. Even plastic items such as bowls and containers can be painted to look as if they are made from expensive metals.

The use of natural colours and finishes is popular. If you cannot afford wood panelling or new floorboards it is easy to paint them, with the added advantage that you can always repaint them at some time if you decide on another scheme.

Foreign travel has had a great influence on lifestyles and decoration. The clean, bright colours found in the Mediterranean and the rich reds and browns of Africa can be adapted to create an unusual or exotic setting in which you can instantly relax. Remember, however, that you might need to lighten the tones for a climate that does not receive such fierce sunlight. As well as using the colours and patterns from exotic places, bring in the textures. Try to match colours to materials. For instance, purples and dark brown wood effects go well together and create a luxurious look.

The world of decorating has no limits. With paint effects you can create whatever look you want. So enjoy the planning and preparations in anticipation of a great result.

BELOW: A tiled look painted in natural earth colours of grey-blue and terracotta. The diamond shapes incorporate a combed effect.

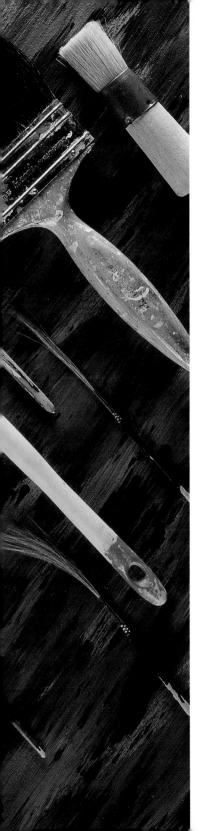

GETTING STARTED

The most important requirement for successful results in paint effects is the proper use of the correct materials and tools. With many of the techniques you can achieve stunning decoration with ordinary household paintbrushes, rollers, sponges and artist's brushes, but specialist equipment is needed for some effects. These items are available in decorators' suppliers and craft shops, where you can also ask for advice on their use.

Choose good quality materials. Make sure that you have the right type of paint suitable for the specific technique you are planning. Read carefully through the steps to check that you have everything you need before you start.

ABOVE: A selection of pigments and stains that can be stirred into water-based paint mediums to create unique colours and textures.

OPPOSITE: You can get a different brush for just about every effect, but special brushes are not always necessary for the different techniques.

BASIC KIT

There are some basic essentials that you will need for decorating. You can add to this equipment gradually as you work on different effects.

- Use a sturdy set of steps to reach the tops of walls and ceilings easily.
- Buy a dust sheet (drop cloth) to protect the floor, furniture and anything precious. Cotton twill dust sheets (drop cloths) are reusable and preferable to the plastic-sheet disposable kind.
- You may sometimes have to remove door furniture or wall fixings, so both Phillips and flat-head screwdrivers are useful. They are also handy for removing paint can lids.
- For general painting, edging and painting woodwork, use household paintbrushes. The most useful sizes are 5cm/2in and 2.5cm/1in. Finer artist's brushes are invaluable for difficult small

spaces and touching up odd areas. Soft sable-haired artist's brushes with rounded edges are best for this use.

- Fill any chipped areas with interior filler (spackle or wood filler), applied with a filling knife, then sand to smooth
- It is sensible to use a paint kettle (pot). Pour the paint into the kettle (pot) a little at a time to make it lighter to hold. Also, in case of accident the spillage will not be so great.
- Use sandpaper to key and prepare previously painted woodwork. It is generally best used with a sanding block for a flatter finish.
- After sanding and prior to painting or staining, use a brush or cloth to dust away the sanded particles.

BELOW: Use a dust sheet to protect the floor from paint spots.

BRUSHES

Numerous types, sizes and qualities of brush are available for different techniques. Stencilling, for instance, is easier if you use a stencil brush, which has short, stiff bristles for stippling the paint. Also, the brush must hold the required quantity of paint, be the correct size for the surface area and made from the right type of hair. Natural hair and bristle brushes are best, but synthetic alternatives are less expensive and can give good results.

Clean your brushes well after use. If you are using oil-based paints and varnishes dip a third of the bristles in the paint and scrape off any excess. Do not leave a loaded brush for more than ten minutes or the paint will start to become tacky. First wipe the brush on to a rag, then rinse off as much of the paint as possible in white spirit (turpentine) or a non-toxic solvent. Scrape off any tough bits and wash the brush thoroughly in washing up liquid (dishwashing detergent) several times until clean. Rinse, shake off the water and reshape.

When using water-based paints or varnishes also make sure that the bristles are not totally covered. If there is a break in the work wash the brush immediately. Scrape off any excess paint, then rinse off under lukewarm water with a little detergent to remove strong colours. Shake off the water and reshape.

- Use a graining brush for certain wood grain effects. These are available in different sizes and with varying "pencils" or clumps of bristles.

- Softener (blending) brushes have soft bristles with rounded ends. Large ones are used for softening (blending) basic finishes and the first layers of faux effects. Smaller ones are used for delicate jobs and fine softening (blending). The best ones are made from badger hair, but are expensive. Use a large soft blusher brush as a good, cheap alternative.

- Dragging brushes are used for woodgraining and dragged effects. They are usually about 5cm/2in or 7.5cm/3in wide. A household brush can be used as an alternative.

- Household paintbrushes are available in a wide variety of sizes. The bristle quality and length tends to vary, and it is best to choose longer bristles. These brushes are used for all basic painting, edging and varnishing.

- Stippling brushes have large blocks of short-cut bristles attached to an angled handle. They are used for stippling, that is, making fine pin-point marks. Stippling brushes are available in various sizes. You can use a masonry brush as an alternative.

- Liner brushes are long, soft brushes used for lining, and for marbling effects. A swordliner (above) is an angled version. Different sizes are available.

ROLLERS AND SPONGES

Many types of specialist rollers are used in decorating. Specific covers are suitable for different surfaces and you can buy rollers designed for particular patterns. A radiator roller is similar, with a long handle for reaching into tight spots. Use much smaller craft and mini-rollers for applying paint in techniques such as stamping. Paint pads (pad painters) can also be useful for clean, flat painting and precise edges and are made from plastic foam, with a short-haired pile inserted into an applicator or handle.

A selection of natural and synthetic sponges is essential for numerous overall decorating techniques, as are lint-free cloths and rags. Each makes its own individual marks, so experiment with the effects.

- Mini-rollers have a cover made from dense foam or pile. Available in several widths, they are used for painting narrow stripes or coating stamps.

- Masonry rollers are generally 23cm/9in wide with a long pile. Use for covering rough surfaces and for roller fidgeting.
- Sheepskin rollers are used for basic quick coverage of flat paint. They are usually available in 18cm/7in and 23cm/9in widths.
- Use a sponge roller as a cheaper alternative to a sheepskin one. Sponge rollers are also available in 18cm/7in and 23cm/9in widths.
- Natural sponges are mostly used for sponging. Synthetic sponges make a more obvious mark than natural sponges, so use natural ones for tight, fine marks and for marbling.
- A chamois, made from real leather, can be scrunched into a ball for ragging. Or use a special ragging chamois, made from strips bound together.

BELOW: *Clockwise from top left; natural sponge, cloth, pinched-out sponge, synthetic sponge, two paint pads, mini-roller, small cellulose sponge, gloss roller, masonry roller, ragging chamois.*

RIGHT: Clockwise from top left; spirit level, long ruler, sanding block, two combs, plumb line, tape measure, heart grainer (graining roller), sanding sponge, craft knife, pencil, selection of sand paper (far right).

BELOW: A triangular comb a and graduated comb.

SPECIALIST TOOLS

There are many items that will make it easier to plan your decoration. For careful measuring and marking before you start, you may need a spirit level (level), long ruler, tape measure and pencil. A plumb line, which consists of a small weight suspended on a fine string, is helpful for marking vertical drops. Masking tape is useful for keeping edges straight and covering light switches and sockets.

For specialist techniques certain tools are needed. Different shapes of rubber combs will give a variety of woodgrain effects. A heart grainer (graining roller) with its moulded surface will enable you to reproduce the characteristics of a particular wood more accurately. For guilding, a gilder's pad is a useful investment and consists of a soft pad surrounded by a screen of parchment to shield gild leaf from draughts. Craft knives can be bought with double-ended blades that

ABOVE: This lighter-weight craft knife has a retractable blade. When it becomes blunt, simply snap off the end for a new edge.

are screwed into the handle and turned or replaced when blunt. Others have a long retractable strip blade that allows you to break off and dispose of the blunt portion. For safety, keep your fingers behind the cutting edge. Never leave the knife within reach of children or where it will be a danger to animals; a cork is a good "lid" to put on the end of the blade. Use craft knives for cutting stencils and stamps.

Keep a supply of different grades of sandpaper, and a sanding block to use with them. An electric (power) sander can also save time on larger jobs. For floorboards a special industrial sander should be hired.

PAINTS

Different paints are suitable for different surfaces and effects and it is important to choose the right paint for the right surface. The techniques and projects in this book suggest the easiest and most effective type to use for each particular effect.

Traditional paints are either water-based or oil-based and generally come in three finishes – matt (flat), satin (mid sheen) and gloss. Most basic wall effects are painted with water-based emulsion (latex) paint since it is easy to apply with a variety of brushes, rollers, sponges and rags. It makes a good base coat, mixes well and several layers can be painted over each other to build up the desired effect. You can tint water-based emulsions (latex) paints with acrylic paints to make your own colours.

Artists' oil colours are frequently used for faux effects. The rich pigments replicate the colours found in different types of wood, marble and other natural surfaces. Oil paints take longer to dry than water-based paints and this can be an advantage if you need to take time in creating a precise effect. They give a more durable finish, but they are a little harder to work with. For a realistic result use enamel paints for metal effects.

Many surfaces benefit from the application of a primer. Primer paints seal and provide a suitable base for paint finishes. They are particularly important if you are working on a porous surface and essential for bare wood. Read the information on the can to make sure you are choosing the correct primer for the specific surface. An undercoat on top of a primer protects the surface further and helps to give a smooth base for the top coat. Oil-based undercoats tend to be used most frequently for painting woodwork.

BELOW: Traditional household paints are available in a tempting array of luscious colours.

HOUSEHOLD PAINTS

These are available in a wide range of finishes from completely matt through varying sheens to high glosses. There is a wealth of colour choice and in many DIY (do-it-yourself) stores you can have an exact colour matched and specially mixed for you. Read the instructions on the can before use to check that it is suitable for your surface. When thinning paint make sure that you are using the correct diluent.

Household paints	Base	Diluent	Uses	Notes
Matt emulsion (latex)	water	water, wallpaper paste acrylic glaze, acrylic varnish, clean with water	basic walls, large choice of colours, flat finish	fast drying, needs varnishing on furniture, marks easily
Silk emulsion (latex)	water	as above	as above faint sheen	fast drying, more hard-wearing than matt, needs varnishing on furniture
Soft sheen	water	as above	kitchens and bathrooms, mid sheen	fast drying, moisture resistant, needs varnishing on furniture
Dead flat oil	oil	linseed oil, white spirit (turpentine), oil glaze, oil varnishes	woodwork, flat/velvet finish	marks easily, not durable
Eggshell	oil	as above	woodwork, faint sheen, furniture	more resistant than above, but still marks
Satin	oil	as above	woodwork, mid sheen, furniture	durable, washable finish
Gloss	oil	as above	woodwork, high sheen, exterior furniture	tough, hard-wearing finish, washable
Primer	oil	not to be diluted, clean with spirits (alcohol)	bare wood	necessary for porous or wood surfaces
Undercoat	oil	not to be diluted, clean with spirits (alcohol)	between the primer and top coat	saves on top coats, choose the right colour
Masonry	water	not to be diluted, clean with water	exterior masonry	limited colours, apply with a suitable roller
Floor	oil	not to be diluted, clean with spirits (alcohol)	floors, light or industrial use	tough, durable, apply with a roller

MODERN PAINTS

Major advances in paint technology have widened the creative possibilities for the home decorator and there is a constant stream of new paints to try. The invention and manufacture of synthetic pigments have resulted in paints that are more permanent in colour and give predictable results. Developments in paint composition have produced modern paints that are easy to apply, cover well and dry quickly. As well as being available in cans they come in many different convenient forms, such as spray aerosols, as a solid block for use with rollers, and in non-drip and one-coat formulas.

Many of the techniques for basic broken-colour and patterned effects described here can be adapted for use on surfaces other than walls and wood. There are now many specialist paints designed for different purposes and materials, such as glass, fabrics and metals. These paints sometimes need to be handled slightly differently from conventional household paints, but experimenting with them is well worth the effort. Stencil paints are designed specifically to use with stencils and come in useful small pots or oil-based stencil sticks, which are easy for blending.

Acrylic and enamel paints have numerous uses. Acrylic paints are water-based, and can be added to other water-based paints or used on their own to paint decorative motifs and flourishes. Enamel paints are oil based, and are suitable for metal and other surfaces that require a particularly tough finish. Both acrylic and enamel paints dry to a durable, washable finish and are available in a massive range of colours, including metallic finishes.

BELOW: A selection of different-coloured paints, including watercolours, stencil paints and acrylics.

TRADITIONAL PAINTS

With the current vogue for restoring old buildings there is renewed enthusiasm for traditional paints made from natural ingredients. Many decorative techniques are designed to give an aged effect and the mellow colours and soft appearance of these paints are ideal. Many of them are earth colours, but they also include some surprisingly bright colours without the more garish characteristics of many modern paints. These are suitable for distressed techniques and antiquing.

Traditional paints are made with natural additives that give a particular finish. Powdered pigments can be used to colour paint, while chalk gives a powdery surface. Use gesso, a white powder prepared with rabbit skin glue, to make a smooth painting surface. Scumble glaze is a transparent medium, made from linseed and other oils, whiting and dryers, which can be used with colour pigments to make various thicknesses of tinted glazes. Milk paints were originally made with milk derivatives and give a dense, matt surface.

RIGHT: This palette of traditional folk paints shows the variety of hues that can be made from natural pigments.

Traditional paints	Base	Diluent	Uses	Notes
Milk paints	water	water wallpaper paste	basic wall large surface areas	dense, matt surface
Distemper (tempera)	powder	water and glue size	woodwork furniture	good for antique effects
Chalk	water	as above	as above	powdery surface
Limewash	water	as above	as above	good for aged effect
Gesso	powder	rabbit skin glue	layered for a smooth finish before gilding or marbling	labour intensive
Powder paint	powder	any	tints anything	can be gritty
Gilt cream	oil	oil varnishes white spirit (turpentine)	easy gilding techniques	metallic colours

BINDERS AND DILUENTS

Pigment needs a binder so that it will adhere to the surface on which it is painted. As well as the binder in the manufacture of the paint there are other binders that you can add to modify its consistency and texture. Diluents and solvents are added to thin the paint and to delay the drying time. Glazes also delay drying and modern products such as acrylic glazes can be used instead of traditional scumble glazes for an easier consistency.

There are many mediums for glazes such as wallpaper paste, linseed oil, PVA (white glue) and dryers that will change the nature of the paint. Solvents such as white spirit can also be used to clean paintbrushes. Make sure you use a diluent or solvent that is suitable for the type of paint you are using.

RIGHT: *A selection of glues and solvents, including wood glue, PVA (white glue), spray adhesive and rubber solution.*

Binders and Diluents	Base	Diluent	Uses	Notes
PVA	water	water	binder for emulsion (latex) washes	makes the mixture more durable
White spirit	oil		paint thinner, brush cleaner	buy in bulk
Linseed oil	oil		medium for powder	lengthy drying
Dryers			add to oil paint to speed drying	
Wallpaper paste	water	water	dilutes emulsions (latex)	retards the drying a little
Acrylic glaze	water	water	as above	retards drying
Scumble glaze	oil	white spirit (turpentine)	medium to suspend colour pigments	difficult to tint to the right quantity
Methylated spirits (methyl alcohol)	oil		softens dried emulsion	
White spirit (Turpentine)	oil		paint thinner, brush cleaner	

Varnishes	Base	Diluent	Uses	Notes
Polyurethane/oil-based	oil	white spirit (turpentine)	strong varnishes in a range of finishes	tough, durable, slow drying
Polyurethane (aerosol)	oil		flat finish	
Acrylic	water	water	range of finishes	not as durable
Acrylic (aerosol)	water		flat finish	
Tinted varnish	oil acrylic	white spirit (turpentine) water	for bare wood, or antiquing paint. Range of colours	slow drying fast drying
Crackle glaze	water	not to be diluted	medium which makes a top coat crackle over a contrasting base coat	reliability of brands varies
Japan gold size	oil	not to be diluted	adhesive medium for gold leaf	quickest drying of the range
Button polish	water	methylated spirits	sealing bare wood	quick drying

VARNISHES

Varnishes seal and protect the surface of the paint, preserving your decoration. There are specific formulas for interior or exterior use and they are usually available in matt (flat), satin (mid sheen) or gloss finishes. Modern varnishes have been developed with a polyurethane or acrylic base. Special mediums such as crackle glaze can be used to produce a cracked protective surface, ideal for an antiqued or distressed effect. Size acts as a sealant and as a base for gilding.

Varnishes are bought in liquid form or as aerosol sprays. Gloss varnish produces a shiny finish, while matt varnish has a flat look. Make sure the varnish you buy is appropriate for interior or exterior use. There are several types of crackle medium on the market, so read the manufacturer's instructions carefully before using one. There are also modern fast-drying or traditional forms of gold size.

Bronze powders are available in several metallic finishes and are used over gold size. You can also use Dutch leaf, which is a less expensive substitute for real gold leaf and gives a good result.

RIGHT: Pots of varnish on a crackle glaze background.

PAINT REMOVAL

Over several years and many applications of paint there can be quite a build-up of layers on a surface. This is not really a problem on walls and ceilings, but on woodwork and metalwork it is a different matter. Attractive mouldings, especially on skirting (base) boards, window frames and architraves, can become clogged and their features indistinct. In addition, moving parts on doors and windows, such as hinges, and the edges of the frames can start to become ill fitting. The answer to this is to strip off the old paint right back to the wood or metal.

Stripping is also the best option if the paintwork looks in poor condition. It may be deeply chipped or have been badly painted, leaving drips and blobs on the surface. In these cases it is unlikely that a new coat of paint will disguise the imperfections on the surface.

You can remove thick layers of old paint with a chemical paint remover in the form of a paste or a liquid stripper that you brush over the paint surface. Wait for the chemicals to react with the paint, then scrape it off with a paint scraper. These chemicals are strong, so read the manufacturer's instructions carefully before applying them and use them properly.

Another way to strip off old paint is to use an electric heat gun. Again, keep safety well in mind and

ABOVE: *The chipped paint on this old chair can easily be removed using one of the techniques shown, and then transformed with a new paint effect.*

wear safety glasses or goggles to protect your eyes. Too much heat can scorch the wood or crack glass if you are not careful. Put the old scrapings in a metal container as you work and cover surrounding areas such as the floor to protect them.

Using liquid stripper

1 Carefully pour some of the stripper into an old glass jar. Then, wearing rubber gloves to protect your hands, brush the stripper on to the painted surface. Leave it until the paint starts to bubble, following the manufacturer's instructions.

2 Scrape off the peeling layers of paint with a paint scraper. Use a shavehook for intricate mouldings.

3 Wash the surface with water or white spirit (turpentine), as recommended by the manufacturer. This will neutralize the chemicals. Then leave to dry.

Using a heat gun

1 Move the heat gun over the surface so that the air stream heats and softens the paint evenly. Scrape off the paint as you work.

2 Be careful not to scorch the wood, especially when working on intricate areas such as mouldings. Use a shavehook to scrape out the paint from these areas.

3 Wearing rubber gloves to protect your hands, rub off any remaining bits of paint with wire (steel) wool soaked in white spirit (turpentine). Work in the direction of the grain of the wood.

4 Clean any particles of paint out of the crevices in the mouldings with a hand vacuum cleaner.

5 Lightly sand the surface of the wood to smooth it. Wipe any dust away with a clean cloth dampened with a little white spirit (turpentine) or a tack cloth.

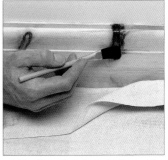

6 Finally, seal any knots in the wood so that the resin cannot escape. Do this by brushing on liquid knotting or shellac. Leave to dry.

Using paste remover

1 These strippers dry slowly and are ideal for stripping intricate mouldings. Wear rubber gloves to protect your hands and apply a thick coating of paste remover to the woodwork.

2 Leave the paste to work, following the manufacturer's instructions. Thick layers of paint will need more time. Use a paint scraper to scrape off the paint. Then wash the surface well with water.

SURFACE PREPARATION

Perhaps the most important factor in achieving a successful result in decorating is to make sure that the surfaces are clean and smooth. Careful preparation can seem rather tedious but it is worth the time spent.

Wash walls with a solution of sugar soap, then rinse them well with clean water. Scrape off any pieces of flaking paint and fix any dents and cracks in the plaster with filler (spackle) and a filler knife. When the filler (spackle) has hardened, sand it smooth with fine-grade sandpaper. Similarly, fix any defects in the woodwork. If knots are showing through the existing paintwork, sand them back and apply knotting or shellac. When dry, paint on primer and undercoat to bring the area level with the rest of the surface of the woodwork.

Clean surfaces such as ceramic tiles, china or glass with soapy water and dry them well with a lint-free cloth. You will then need to use specialist paints, as emulsion (latex) and acrylic paints will not adhere well to these smooth surfaces.

Preparing woodwork

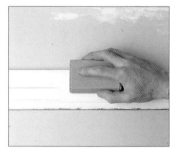  

1 Sand down the surface with fine-grade sandpaper over a sanding block. This smoothes the surface of old bits of paint and provides a key to which the new paint can adhere.

2 Wash the paintwork with water and detergent to make sure that it is completely clean of grease and dust. Then rinse it well with clean water so that there is no detergent left to prevent the new paint from adhering.

3 Dampen a clean cloth with white spirit (turpentine) or a tack cloth to remove any dust from intricate mouldings and corners.

Filling defects in woodwork

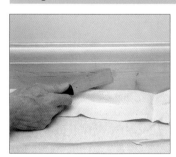  

1 With a putty knife, stop any holes, dents or cracks in the wood. Use ordinary filler (spackle) for wood that will be painted, and tinted wood filler for wood that will be varnished.

2 Work the filler into corners with your finger or the corner of a putty knife. Smooth off any excess or edges before the filler dries.

3 When the filler is hard, sand it down so that it is flush with the surface of the wood. The best way to do this is by using fine-grade sandpaper wrapped around a sanding block.

Preparing shiny surfaces

1 Wash shiny surfaces such as tile, china or glass with soapy water. Then rinse them well.

2 Wipe them with a clean cloth dampened with methylated spirits to make sure no grease remains.

Filling cracks in plaster

1 Rake out loose material from the crack with the corner of a putty knife. Undercut the edges of the crack slightly to provide an edge to which the filler (spackle) can grip.

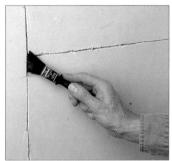

2 Use an old paintbrush to brush out any debris and dust. You could also use the crevice fitment of a vacuum cleaner for this job.

3 Use a water spray to dampen the plaster around the crack so that the filler will not dry too quickly and cause further cracks.

4 Mix up some powdered filler (spackle) on a board, following the manufacturer's instructions. Or use ready-mixed filler if you prefer.

5 Press the filler into the crack with a filling knife. Draw the blade of the knife across the filled crack and then along it. The filler should stand slightly proud of the surrounding surface.

6 When the filler is completely hard sand it smooth so that it is level with the surrounding surface. Do this with a piece of fine-grade sandpaper wrapped around a sanding block.

USING BRUSHES AND ROLLERS

Paint is applied using brushes, rollers or paint pads (pad painters). Brushes are available in a range of widths, so choose one that is suitable for the surface you are painting – for instance, use a narrow brush for the glazing bars of a window. For large areas use a wide brush, or a roller for fast coverage.

If you wish to paint with a previously used brush that has not been kept covered, wash it well first to remove any bits and pieces. Leave it to dry before using it. Check that the ferrule of the brush is securely fixed to the handle and clean off any traces of rust with wire (steel) wool or sandpaper.

Rollers are excellent for large flat areas. Choose a suitable sleeve depending on whether you are painting on smooth plaster or a textured surface. You may also need to use a brush in corners where the roller will not fit. Paint pads (pad painters) cover less quickly than brushes or rollers, but they apply paint more smoothly.

Preparing the paint

1 Wipe the lid of the can first to get rid of any dust. Prise the lid off gently with a wide lever so that you do not damage the lip.

2 Pour some paint into a clean paint kettle (pot) or bucket. You will find a container with a handle easier to work with and replacing the lid on the can will keep the rest of the paint fresher.

3 Use up old paint by first removing any skin from the top, then straining it through a clean piece of cheesecloth (muslin) or an old, fine silk stocking.

Using a brush

1 When using a new brush for the first time remove any stray hairs by working it vigorously across the palm of your hand.

2 Use small or medium brushes by placing your fingers on one side of the ferrule and your thumb on the other. This gives you better control.

3 Hold wide brushes by the handle or your hand will quickly become tired.

Using a roller

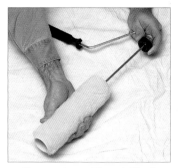

1 Choose a sleeve with a suitable pile and place on the sprung metal cage.

2 Pour the paint into a roller tray until it just overlaps the deeper part.

3 Paint a band in the corners and angles where the roller will not fit.

4 Load the roller by rolling it down the slope of the tray into the paint.

5 Apply the paint by using the roller in overlapping diagonal movements.

6 Blend the sections together by working in parallel to the edges.

Applying the paint

1 Dip only a third of the bristles into the paint. If you put too much paint on the brush you will cause paint to run down the handle or make drips.

2 Tie a piece of wire or string across the top of the paint kettle (pot) or bucket so that you can scrape off excess paint against it.

3 Use long sweeping strokes to apply the paint, working in the direction of the grain, until the paint on the brush is used. Then reload with paint and apply it to the next section.

4 Blend the two sections together with short, light strokes. Paint edges and corners by letting the brush run off the edge and repeating the process on the opposite edge.

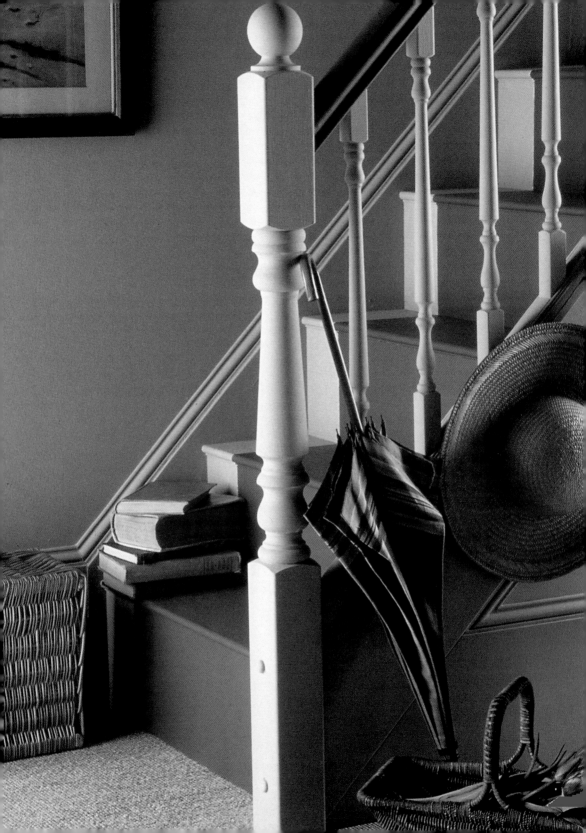

USING COLOUR

Colour can have tremendous impact in our homes. The colours we choose for our surroundings reflect our personalities, lifestyles, travels and interests. They set the scene for an atmosphere of relaxation or stimulation, for quiet contemplation or family get-togethers and parties.

We live in a world that contains millions of natural colours. Today, using synthetic dyes and stainers, we can match almost any colour found in nature in the form of paint, fabrics and other materials. An understanding of the visual effects that these different colours can produce will help you plan creative and successful decorating schemes.

ABOVE: For special effects watercolour, acrylic and special stencil paints are invaluable. The colour palette is more restricted than with household paints, but you can have great fun mixing your own shades.

OPPOSITE: The coolness or vibrancy of a colour has a major effect on the appearance of a room. Here, pale blue walls are prevented from looking cold by being teamed with warm yellow and orange colours.

COLOUR TERMINOLOGY

K nowing some of the generally accepted theories of how colour works will enable you to use colours to their best advantage and for particular purposes. Artists, designers and decorators use precise terms to describe colours and the differences between them.

Red, yellow and blue are known as primary colours. These are colours that cannot be produced from a combination of other pigments. Mixing two primary colours produces the secondary colours: red and yellow results in orange, yellow and blue in green, and blue and red in violet.

Placing primary and secondary colours in a circle in their appropriate positions forms a colour wheel. Tertiary colours can then be produced by mixing a primary colour with a secondary colour that is next to it. For instance, red mixed with violet gives red-violet. Experiment by making your own colour wheel, mixing adjacent colours for an infinite variety.

ABOVE: Colours that are immediately opposite each other on the colour wheel are termed complementary. For example, violet is complementary to yellow, and green to red. These opposites enhance each other and make each appear more intense. Here green is painted next to a tint of its complementary red (pink). The colours really seem to glow against each other.

BELOW: Tints are made by adding white to a colour, and shades by adding black. These pastel stripes show tints of colours. They are all also similar in tone - they have the same amount of light or dark.

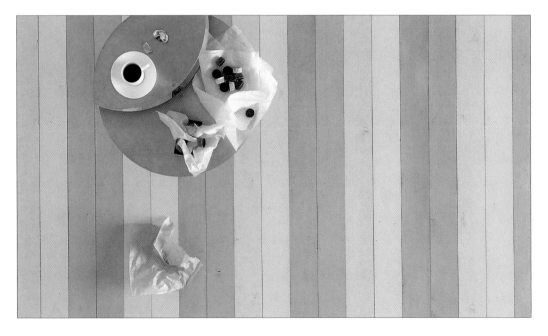

ABOVE: *Colours that are near each other on the colour wheel are called harmonious. Having elements in common, they relate and work well together. For instance, the swatches of main colour shown here work well with the dashes of colour painted below them.*

BELOW: *Contrasting colours can also give a dramatic effect. These are colours that are not related at all, but create impact because they are of the same tone. The main colour swatches shown here are matched in intensity by the dashes of colour painted below them.*

DENSITY OF COLOUR

The amount of colour used in a room and where it is placed can create a dramatic or a subtle effect. Use it in large areas to create an overall atmosphere or in selected small areas to emphasize particular features. Clever use of colour can appear to change the proportions of a room, making it appear bigger or smaller than it really is. Remember that your furniture and fabrics are all part of the same scheme. Be careful not to use too many colours or the effect will be unbalanced.

LEFT: The more intense a colour is, the more we notice it. Adding a gloss finish or glazing surfaces can make them look much brighter. This chair is varnished, making it stand out as well as protecting the distressed paint effect.

BELOW: It is generally accepted that colours towards the red end of the spectrum appear to advance. However, an intense red used in a large area can look overpowering. Here, a dramatic effect is produced by using areas of different reds, allowing the eye to move constantly forwards and backwards.

ABOVE: Towards the other end of the spectrum from red, blue is a colour that seems to recede. It is therefore useful to use in decorating schemes where you want to increase the feeling of space. Here intense blue and yellow accessories balance each other visually on the sill, but the pale blue shutters beyond lead the eye out of the window, making the room seem bigger.

COLOUR AND LIGHT

When you are choosing paints or coloured materials for your home make sure that you look at the colours in natural daylight at different times of the day. A colour in a room facing the sun varies from morning to night, while a colour in a room that does not receive much, if any, direct sunlight remains largely consistent. Colours can look quite different in artificial light too.

Seasons and geographical location also have an influence on our impressions of colour. A bright colour that you see on vacation under a glaring Caribbean sun may not work as well in your own living room, but you may be able to modify it. You can also tone colours down by adding a little of the complementary colour.

RIGHT: This Indian-style room is decorated with just two bright primary colours – red and yellow. However, the jewel-like scarlet is balanced by the natural ochre colour so that the effect is rich and warm rather than garish. The sheen finish on the walls reflects the light in the room and the sheer curtain fabric gently diffuses light coming through the window.

COLOUR AND TEXTURE

Textures can emphasize the general effect given by colour. We associate hard, glossy finishes with streamlining and efficiency and so they tend to look cold, especially when used with colours in the blue range. Warm-looking traditional surfaces such as soft, grainy woods and rich, textured fabrics that suggest age and reliability enhance the effect of reds, oranges and browns. General paint effects such as combing and rag rolling can be lightly or heavily textured, so when you are choosing colours think carefully about the overall effect you want to create.

RIGHT: Colour and texture combine here to produce a restful environment, yet one full of visual interest. The walls have been dry-brushed in green and purple – two shades that always work well together – creating an illusion of texture, while the grapevine border was made using a bought stencil.

BELOW: Everything in this room speaks of warmth and comfort. The faux-effect wood panelling sets the scene, and the soft, grained effect is enhanced by the cream walls. Furniture with traditional coverings such as leather and rush are timeless and lend an air of comfort.

NATURAL SHADES

The colours and textures of nature can be brought into home decoration and used over and over again to add a calming note. They are surfaces that are always interesting and diverse, yet complement any environment and style, old or new, classic or modern. The shades you choose may be bright or subtle.

Greens and blues are perennial favourites in home decoration, either used singly in toning shades or together. Browns, soft oranges, buttermilk yellows, beiges and creams are also natural colours that harmonize well in the home; they are often seen in country-style kitchens, reinforcing the sense of warmth and comfort. Neutral colour schemes allow you to use a mixture of textures for visual variety. They can also act as a foil to small areas of bright colours that can be changed from time to time to give a different accent to a room.

RIGHT: These pale greens and blues in a matt (flat) finish suggest the places in which we find escape in the heat of summer, such as cool water or shady areas. The walls are defined by clean white lines of matt skirting (base) board, and the wood-washed floor looks as if it has faded in the sun.

RIGHT: This entire scheme relies on a neutral palette of off-white, accessorized with metal furniture and gold-accented ornaments. The wall motifs were created using a stamp dipped in a mixture of stone white and interior filler (spackle) and add subtle highlights and texture to the wall.

COLOUR GROUPS

You can achieve stunning effects with monochrome schemes using colours of one hue, or black and white, or black and cream, or the many tones of grey that can be mixed from these combinations. Other greys can be mixed by using exact proportions of two complementary colours, so they can be used as a neutralizing effect in conjunction with a bright decorative palette.

Various browns also work well together visually, since they are based on earth pigments and thus have a natural affinity with each other. They are good for rustic looking decorating schemes, since these are the colours that would most commonly have been used in country interiors.

RIGHT: Try seeing how many tones of black, brown and grey you can make by adding water to thin down the pigment. The addition of white or cream gives further ranges of colours. These can be combined in a scheme or used as neutral background or relief with other colours.

ABOVE: The aged look of this painted brown door makes a backdrop to a palette of warm earth colours in the form of items made from natural materials. These include iron, terracotta, buff clay, hessian, raffia and wood.

OPPOSITE: This is a powerful 'no colour' scheme. It combines strong bands of cream with white painted panels defined by unusual greys. The look is softened by the textures of white cotton sheets and a cream quilted bedspread.

RIGHT: Here, soft greys ranging towards white are used for a restful, but interesting, scheme. The matt painted effects of the wood-washed floor and distressed chair are enhanced by the textures of velvet, sequins, satin ribbons and silk muslin.

YELLOW, ORANGE AND RED

Red is a very versatile colour, able to conjure up many different moods. Used at full strength in its purest form it is dramatic and powerful. Yellow is the colour of sunshine and summer. Its visual warmth is intensified by the addition of red to make glowing oranges that cheer the heart. Use yellow and orange in rooms that receive little natural light to give them an instant lift. You can choose clear pastel tints for a gentle ambience or bright hues to create a bolder effect. The lighter yellows tend to give a fresh look that can appear surprisingly cool, while the redder oranges can look even more dramatic teamed with complementary blues.

LEFT: *Mix a variety of yellows to achieve colours that similarly range from clean bright oranges to burnt and brown tones.*

RIGHT: *Painted in yellow, this kitchen has a sunny feel, slightly cooled by touches of blue, violet and white. The fresh, country-style gingham effect on the wall is quickly achieved by painting two lines at a time from a roller with the middle section cut out.*

BELOW: *Here a richly worked orange-brown wall links a number of elements in different colours from the same part of the colour wheel – yellow curtains, bright red accessories, tan cushions and a cream sofa.*

BELOW: *This lovely old folk chest is decorated with freehand traditional flower motifs in red and brown. Warm red is balanced by creamy yellow panels and the colours are enhanced by just a little soft blue from the cooler part of the colour wheel.*

PINK, LILAC AND PEACH

Red is a very strong colour in its purest forms. Yet, when diluted to its minimum, or added to white, red gives the softest of pinks for a sophisticated dining room or a new-born's nursery. Add it to blue and relax into a completely new world of lilacs, mauves and violets. Add it to pale yellow and you can enjoy gentle shades of orange from the palest warm beige to a soft terracotta.

RIGHT: These pinks, mauves and oranges are based on red mixed with white. The more intense colours in the range work well with similarly intense colours such as lime green or turquoise.

OPPOSITE: Here different shades of pink have been combined to produce a fresh and modern colour scheme – ice-cream pastel pink on the walls harmonizes with the mauve-blue wash, peach towel and bright fuschia soap.

BELOW: A diluted red used as a pink wood wash gives a rosy tinge to old floorboards. Some of the natural colour of the wood is allowed to show through, adding yellow-orange tints to the effect.

BLUES AND GREENS

Blues and greens are relaxing to look at and to live with. They are familiar to us because they make up so much of our world. The sky displays a vast area of constantly changing blues, as does the sea. Green, of course, is the colour of plant growth, from soft greyish leaves to bright yellow-green buds. Blues and greens in their myriad variants seem to bring a breath of outdoors into the home. Use pale blues and greens for a cool, airy feel or deep, brilliant tones for a more exotic effect.

LEFT: Blue is closely related to green, needing the addition of just a little yellow to produce a colour that displays new characteristics. Although from the cool part of the colour wheel, these colours can appear quite warm if a warm yellow or red is added to blue.

OPPOSITE: A vivid yellow-green combined with brilliant white paintwork brings a fresh feel of spring. Small silver diamond motifs on the wall keep the green from looking too dense.

LEFT: A blue colourwashed shade on the walls is accented with bright blue and orange in a hand-painted tile effect. The whole scheme is simple and fresh.

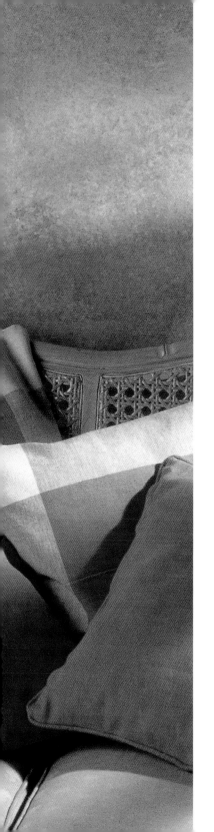

CREATING THE EFFECTS

The following pages show how to create the paint effects that are used later in the projects. They also provide a wealth of further techniques that will inspire you to try out new decorating ideas in your home. All the methods are described in clear steps so that you can produce stunning results with the simplest of instructions. The effects range from basic background techniques, then progress on to planning patterned effects and painting a variety of faux finishes. Read through each one before you start it so that you know what it entails and what you will need in terms of materials and equipment.

ABOVE: Sometimes the simplest effects work best – for a really contemporary feel, combine a beechwood effect on the table with a broad stripe on the wall behind.

OPPOSITE: The soft muted shade on the walls perfectly complements the light wood furniture and the green and burnt-orange cushions.

BASIC FINISHES

The techniques demonstrated in this section are
traditional paint effects, most of which can be used
for all-over impact. They are mainly suitable for
decorating large areas quickly and with ease.
Several, such as distressing, antiquing and
lacquering, are ideal for putting your own personal
stamp on furniture, while others, such as crackle
glaze and gilding, will enable you to transform
small items and home accessories into something
decorative and special.

COLOURWASHING

Colourwashing is usually done with a broad brush using emulsion (latex) paint diluted with water, wallpaper paste and emulsion glaze to make a mixture known as a wash. The effect varies depending on the consistency of the paint mixture and the method of applying the colour. Here, two different tools are used: a large household paintbrush and a synthetic sponge.

COLOURWASHING ONE LAYER

Colourwashing is a quick and flexible effect and is particularly good at disguising small imperfections. Generally, a good guide for mixing is to use 50 per cent emulsion (latex) paint with 50 per cent wallpaper paste. The stronger the paint colour, and the paler the basecoat, the stronger the effect.

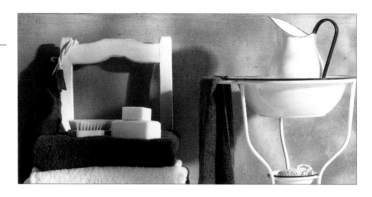

ABOVE RIGHT: The broad strokes used in colour washes work well in bathrooms where the humidity can sometimes leave marks on flat, plain walls.

Using a brush

1 Using a paint kettle (pot), mix 50 per cent emulsion (latex) paint with 50 per cent wallpaper paste (premixed to a thin solution). Using at least a 10cm/4in brush (up to 15cm/6in), dip the tip into the mixture and wipe off the excess on the side of the kettle (pot). Add the first dashes on to the wall, well spaced.

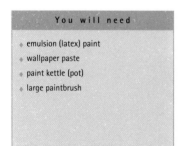

You will need

- emulsion (latex) paint
- wallpaper paste
- paint kettle (pot)
- large paintbrush

2 Without adding more paint, brush out these dashes in random directions using broad sweeping strokes.

3 Continue along the wall adding a little more paint as you go and using quite a dry brush to blend the joins (seams).

Using a sponge

1 Mix the paint in a paint kettle (pot) using 50 per cent emulsion (latex) paint and 50 per cent wallpaper paste (premixed to a thin solution). Dip the side of the sponge in to the kettle, scrape off the excess on the side of the kettle and add random dashes on to the wall.

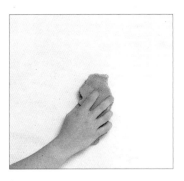

2 Using broad strokes, smear the paint across the wall in varying directions in a large wiping motion.

3 Continue the next section by adding more paint and soften the joins (seams).

COLOURWASHING ONE LAYER

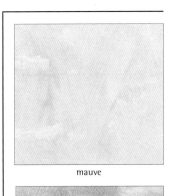

mauve

burnt orange

lime green

stone blue

deep mustard

terracotta

COLOURWASHING TWO LAYERS

This is done in the same way as colourwashing one layer but once the first layer is dry a second colour is applied on top. This layering will soften the overall effect of the brush or sponge marks. Try different colour variations and layering combinations.

You will need

♦ emulsion (latex) paint in two colours
♦ wallpaper paste
♦ paint kettle (pot)
♦ large paintbrush

When the first layer is completely dry repeat step 1 using a second colour of paint.

Using a sponge

1 Mix the paint in a paint kettle (pot) using 50 per cent emulsion (latex) paint and 50 per cent wallpaper paste (premixed to a thin solution). Apply with a sponge using random strokes. Continue over the whole surface.

2 When completely dry apply a second colour with a sponge in the same way as in step 1.

3 Add more paint and soften the joins (seams) as you work.

Using a brush

1 Mix the paint in a paint kettle (pot) using 50 per cent emulsion (latex) paint and 50 per cent wallpaper paste (premixed to a thin solution). Apply with random strokes to the wall, varying the direction as you go. Continue over the whole surface.

3 Add more paint and soften the joins (seams). The overall colourwash effect will be much softer than with using just one colour.

You will need

♦ emulsion (latex) paint in two colours
♦ wallpaper paste
♦ paint kettle (pot)
♦ synthetic sponge

COLOURWASHING TWO LAYERS

camel under cream	purple under mauve	jade green under pale green
blue under cream	burnt orange under mustard	red under pale yellow

LEFT: Colour-washing is ideal for covering large surfaces quickly and easily. By mixing two shades of blue, one darker than the other, a strong, Mediterranean hue can be achieved.

SPONGING

Sponging is a simple technique that is perfect for the beginner because of the ease and speed with which large areas can be covered. It literally consists of dipping a sponge into undiluted paint, scraping off the excess and dabbing on to the wall. Varied effects can be made by using either a synthetic sponge or a natural sponge. A natural sponge will produce smaller, finer marks while heavier marks can be created with a synthetic sponge, such as a car washing sponge, by pinching out small chunks from it. You may find edges and corners are a bit tricky with a larger sponge, so use a smaller piece of sponge for these.

SPONGING ONE LAYER

Much of the effect you achieve with this technique relies on your choice of colour over a base coat. Experiment with colour variations and layering.

You will need
◆ emulsion (latex) paint
◆ natural sponge

Using a natural sponge

1 Dip the sponge into the paint and scrape off the excess, ensuring that there are no blobs left on the sponge. Lightly dab on the paint, alternating the angle of application.

2 Add more paint, continuing to work over the surface. Fill in any gaps and make sure the overall pattern is similar.

Using a synthetic sponge

1 Take an ordinary synthetic sponge and pinch chunks out using your forefinger and thumb. Do this especially along the edges so that there is no sharp line left, and also remove pieces from the middle. Dip the sponge in the paint, scrape off the excess and dab on to the wall in alternating angles.

You will need
◆ emulsion (latex) paint
◆ synthetic sponge

2 Continue over the surface, making sure the pattern is even and filling in any gaps.

SPONGING

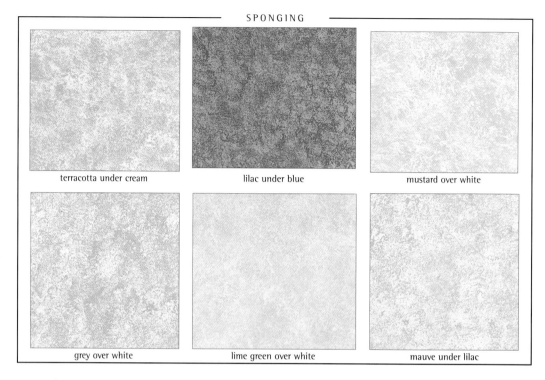

terracotta under cream

lilac under blue

mustard over white

grey over white

lime green over white

mauve under lilac

SPONGING TWO LAYERS

The technique is the same as for sponging one layer, but the overall effect is deepened by the addition of another colour.

Using a natural sponge

You will need

- emulsion (latex) paint in two colours
- natural sponge

1 Apply a single layer by dipping the sponge into the paint, then scrape off the excess and dab on to the wall for an even pattern. Making the pattern even is not quite so important when applying two colours because the second layer will soften the effect. Allow the surface to dry completely.

2 Wash the sponge out and dry it thoroughly. Dip it into the second colour paint, scraping off the excess as before and dabbing on to the surface. Do not over-apply it, however, as you must make sure the first colour isn't totally covered.

Using a synthetic sponge

1 Pinch out the sponge to remove the harsh edges and large chunks in the middle. Dip into the paint, scrape off the excess and dab on to the wall in varying angles. Allow the surface to dry completely.

2 Wash the sponge out and ensure that it is completely dry before applying the second colour as before by dipping in the paint, scraping off the excess and dabbing on to the wall. Use a lighter movement so that the first colour is not totally covered.

You will need

◆ emulsion (latex) paint in two colours
◆ synthetic sponge

RIGHT: Sponge a plain lamp base to make a bold decorative statement.

SPONGING LAYERS

orange, red and yellow

pale green, jade and grey

turquoise and lime green

pale terracotta and yellow

purple and grey

cornflower blue and grey

DRAGGING

A special dragging brush is often used to achieve this effect, but it can also be done with a household paintbrush or even the end of a sponge, though the coarseness of the tool used will determine the finished effect. The actual technique is very simple – the brush is pulled down over wet paint in a clean line to produce a striped effect. These lines must be unbroken, so doing a full-height room may prove extremely difficult. To overcome this a horizontal band can be added, perhaps as a dado (chair) rail, which will break up the height of the room and allow a full reach of the brush within each of the sections.

1 Draw a baseline. Mix emulsion (latex) paint with 50 per cent wallpaper paste (premixed to a thin solution) in a paint kettle (pot) and brush on in a lengthways band, slightly overlapping the baseline. Work on one small section at a time, about 15-25cm/6-10in wide.

2 Dampen the dragging brush with the wash before use, as it will initially take off too much paint if used dry. Then take the brush in one hand and flatten the bristles out with your other hand. Pull the brush down in as straight a motion as possible. This will create deep groove lines in the paint mixture.

3 Brush on more paint mixture, joining up with the last one and slightly overlapping.

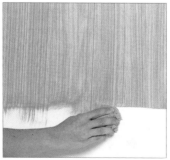

4 Drag straight over the join (seam) and continue dragging.

5 Once this top section has been done, take a damp cloth and, pulling along the pencil line, remove the excess paint.

6 Drag in a horizontal motion across the bottom of the baseline, creating subtle stripes in a different direction.

RIGHT: To achieve this effect on a simple wooden picture frame, paint a layer of pale orange emulsion (latex) on the frame, masking the corners to create crisp angles. Then paint on a second coat in a deeper shade and drag the brush through this layer before allowing it to dry.

DRAGGING

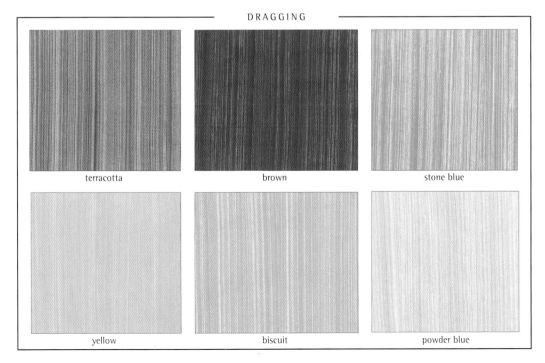

terracotta

brown

stone blue

yellow

biscuit

powder blue

DRY BRUSHING

This is a technique that uses very little paint. The tips of the bristles of the brush are literally dipped into the paint kettle (pot) and as much paint as possible is removed. Then the brush is held almost parallel to the wall and, with little pressure applied, the paint is brushed on in varying directions. The technique is similar to colourwashing but the paint does not totally cover the surface and creates a more textured effect. However, it also emphasizes any dents or imperfections in the surface and you should consider whether this technique is appropriate before application. It suits a rustic setting, perhaps in a kitchen or outdoor room.

DRY BRUSHING WITH ONE COLOUR

As with colourwashing, you can apply just one layer of colour. To enhance the textured look make sure that the base coat remains visible underneath.

RIGHT: Use this technique over bare wood, such as this kitchen stool in white.

You will need
◆ emulsion (latex) paint
◆ wallpaper paste
◆ paint kettle (pot)
◆ large paintbrush

1 Dip the tip of a large household paintbrush into undiluted paint. Scrape off as much as possible and brush on to the wall in varying directions, covering about 2,000 sq cm/2 sq ft.

2 Continue working in the same way, only adding more paint to the brush when there is hardly any paint left at all. But do ensure that the base coat still appears underneath.

3 Add a little more paint to the surface until the whole effect is evened up and slightly softened. The more the surface is brushed over the softer the effect.

DRY BRUSHING WITH TWO COLOURS

Adding a second layer of colour slightly deepens the overall effect. Make sure the amount of paint going on to the wall is actually lighter than the first coat, as the base coat and the first colour still need to be visible.

1 When the first colour is dry add a second colour, working in the same way.

2 Add more paint all over so that the effect is even.

3 Go back over the entire surface filling any gaps or holes that have been created. This is often best achieved by standing as far back as possible and viewing the wall as a whole.

You will need

- emulsion (latex) paint in two colours
- wallpaper paste
- paint kettle (pot)
- large paintbrush

DRY BRUSHING

biscuit over white

lime green over white

powder blue over white

cornflower blue under white

deep mauve under pale mauve

red under camel

STIPPLING

Stippling gives a delicate and subtle finish. The technique consists of making fine, pinpoint marks over a wash of emulsion (latex) paint and it creates a soft, mottled effect. However, it can be quite tiring to do as the brush has to be dabbed over the surface many times applying a good amount of even pressure. A two-man team can speed up the process with one person applying the paint and the other stippling the surface.

A specialist (specialty) stippling brush is useful as it provides a large area of compact bristles, but it is not essential. A wallpaper pasting brush or large household paintbrush is suitable and will create a more obvious stippled effect because of the coarseness of the bristles. Whichever large brush you use, you will also need a small household brush (probably about 2.5cm/1in) to achieve the effect in the edges and corners.

You will need

- emulsion (latex) paint
- paint kettle (pot)
- wallpaper paste
- household paintbrush

Using a household paintbrush

1 Mix up a wash of 50 per cent emulsion (latex) paint and 50 per cent wallpaper paste (premixed to a thin solution) in a paint kettle (pot). Brush on a thin, even coat of the mixture over an area of about 2,000 sq cm/2 sq ft.

2 Take the brush and dab over the surface with the tips of the bristles until the effect is even all over.

3 Continue stippling over the surface until there are no obvious joins (seams) and the whole effect looks soft and even.

LEFT: *Dark green acrylic is stippled over light green on this picture frame.*

Using a stippling brush

1 Mix 50 per cent emulsion (latex) paint with 50 per cent wallpaper paste (premixed to a thin solution). Brush a thin, even coat of the mixture over an area of about 2,000 sq cm/2 sq ft.

2 Dab over the surface with a stippling brush. Continue dabbing over the area with the stippling brush until the entire effect is even and pleasing to you.

3 Repeat the process until the whole area is finished.

STIPPLING

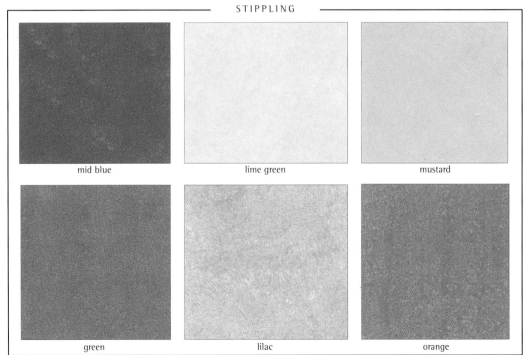

mid blue	lime green	mustard
green	lilac	orange

ROLLER FIDGETING

This is a quick and simple technique and consists of pouring two undiluted emulsion (latex) paint colours into a roller tray, one at each side. You will find that the two paints will sit quite happily together and do not instantly mix. Then, a long pile masonry roller is skimmed over the surface of these colours until a good thick coat is applied. This is rolled on to the wall at varying angles. Little pressure is needed as the texture of the roller and the two colours will do most of the work.

The more the paint is rollered on, the more the colours will blend together, giving an overall dramatic effect. The impact of the effect will depend on the strength of the colours that are used and how many times the wet paint is rollered over. For the edges and corners use a 2.5cm/1in brush and stipple the surface so that it blends in to the rest of the effect. This technique covers a large area in a short time and is simple enough for even the most novice of decorators.

Interesting colour combinations to use are red and camel, powder blue and cream, yellow and cream, pale and dark mauve, mid (medium) blue and mid (medium) green, purple and shocking pink, terracotta and pale terracotta, and sage green and mint.

1 Pour two colours into each side of the pool of the roller tray. Apply a thick coat from here onto the roller so that it will look like a two-tone effect. Apply the roller to the wall at varying angles using short strokes.

2 Continue to work without applying any more paint to the roller until the colours are slightly softened together. The roller can be turned round so that you do not end up with a slightly striped effect on the wall. Keep the angles as random as possible.

3 Go over the whole effect with the roller to soften it. Add more paint when starting another area. Stand back every so often just to make sure there is no heavy concentration of one colour in any particular area.

You will need

- paint tray
- emulsion (latex) paint in two colours
- long pile masonry roller
- 2.5cm/1in household paintbrush

OPPOSITE: Using a mixture of muted colours on your roller looks good in a living room and helps to creates a calm place in which to relax and entertain.

ROLLER FIDGETING

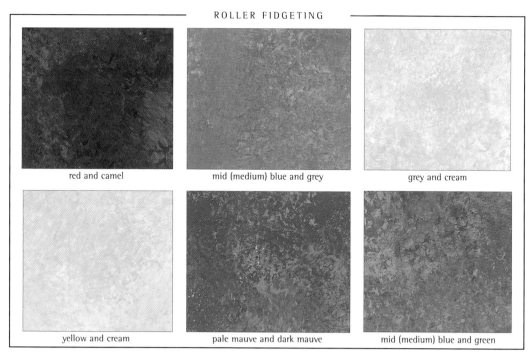

red and camel

mid (medium) blue and grey

grey and cream

yellow and cream

pale mauve and dark mauve

mid (medium) blue and green

RAGGING

Ragging can be done in two ways – ragging on and ragging off – and both techniques are as simple as they sound. With ragging on you dab the rag into the paint then dab on to the surface. With ragging off you brush paint on to the surface and then use a rag to remove some of the paint, leaving a ragged print.

The recommended "rag" to use is a chamois, as it creates a definite print, though you can use most types of cloths for a particular effect. When using either of the techniques, the chamois leather should be periodically squeezed out, as too much paint will result in blobs and drips on the wall.

RAGGING ON

This technique is as simple as sponging, but leaves a sharper effect. Again, the choice of colour you rag on over a base coat will dictate the impact of the finished effect. Make sure that the ragging is evenly applied.

You will need
◆ emulsion (latex) paint
◆ wallpaper paste
◆ paint kettle (pot)
◆ roller tray
◆ chamois

1 Mix 50 per cent emulsion (latex) paint with 50 per cent wallpaper paste in a paint kettle (pot). Pour into a roller tray. Scrunch up a chamois, dip it into the paint and dab off the excess, then dab the "rag" on to the wall.

2 Continue rescrunching the chamois and dipping it into the paint as before, then dabbing it on to the wall until the wall is covered evenly.

LEFT: Ragging can also be used to create a patterned effect, as on this colourful harlequin screen.

RAGGING OFF

Ragging off produces a stronger effect, like crumpled fabric.

1 Mix 50 per cent emulsion (latex) with 50 per cent wallpaper paste (premixed to a thin solution) in a paint kettle (pot). Brush the wash on over a large area.

2 Take a chamois, scrunch it up into a ball and dab on to the wall to gently remove small areas of paint. Vary the angles with each dab. Wring out the chamois and scrunch it up again at any time when it is a bit too heavy with paint or the ragging marks are looking a little too repetitive.

3 Continue working over the surface until the entire effect is even. If you find you are taking off too much paint, apply more immediately with a brush and then dab the chamois over the surface again as before.

RAGGING

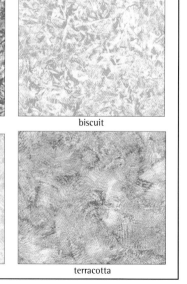

mid (medium) blue

deep mauve

biscuit

grey

pale mauve

terracotta

COMBING

Combing is an easy technique that also enables you to use your own imagination to create a variety of patterns. The basic method involves pulling a comb through paint that is still wet, in order to give a lined effect. A specialist (specialty) rubber combing tool is a recommended purchase, as it is sturdy as well as being flexible and washable, but you could make your own comb if necessary using stiff cardboard with teeth cut out of it. The number of patterns that can be produced is almost endless but you should practise each effect beforehand to test the ability to reproduce it over and over again. Make sure that the surface you are working on is totally smooth or the comb will jump and miss sections and the overall effect will look messy.

BASIC COMBING

Basic combing involves pulling the comb down in a straight line. When straight combing you must also remember that the comb needs to be pulled down in a clean sweep. You may find it difficult to comb an entire wall by pulling the comb all the way from the top to the bottom in one stroke. A straight combing effect is more suitable for a small area.

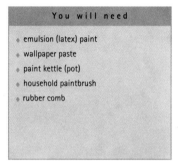

You will need

- emulsion (latex) paint
- wallpaper paste
- paint kettle (pot)
- household paintbrush
- rubber comb

1 Mix 75 per cent emulsion (latex) with 25 per cent wallpaper paste (premixed to a thin solution) in a paint kettle (pot) and brush on in a vertical direction.

2 Hold the comb at a 90-degree angle to the wall and pull down in a straight line. If the comb wobbles or you make a mistake, just brush more paint over it immediately and rework the combing in the same way as before.

LEFT: A chequerboard floor is given the extra effect of a combed texture.

MAKING PATTERNS

Practise continuous patterns and broken patterns where you lift the comb from the surface at regular intervals. There are endless variations you can try, and they work particularly well if you combine them with contrasting colours. Always allow the base coat to dry before applying the top coat and comb the pattern immediately, while the paint is still easy to manipulate.

Vertical and horizontal stripes.

Long wave using parallel strokes.

Scrolls using elongated "S" shapes.

Chequerboard made by crossing vertical and horizontal lines at regular intervals.

COMBING

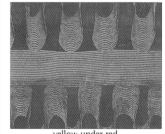
yellow under red

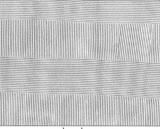
camel under cream

grey under green

grey under powder blue

cream under yellow

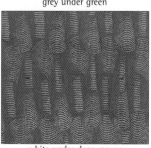
white under deep mauve

FROTTAGE

Frottage consists of brushing a wash on to the wall or surface and then taking either a piece of paper or plastic, placing it over the top while the paint is still wet, scrunching it slightly and then lifting it away. Once removed, the paper or plastic leaves quite an obvious folded-fabric effect. The amount of diluted paint mixture is integral to the success of this technique. Too much will result in the paint dripping with only some patches picking up the effect, while too little will not show any print at all. A good even coat should be applied – practice will help you gauge the amount – and the surface can be brushed over with paint mixture again if the first attempt is not as successful as you would like.

USING PAPER

As the newspaper is absorbent, it will remove more of the paint than if you use plastic. Replace the paper with a clean piece as often as is necessary.

You will need
◆ emulsion (latex) paint
◆ wallpaper paste
◆ paint kettle (pot)
◆ household paintbrush
◆ newspaper

1 Mix 50 per cent emulsion (latex) paint with 50 per cent wallpaper paste (premixed to a thin solution) in a paint kettle (pot) and brush on the mixture in a large area of about 3,000 sq cm/3 sq ft.

2 Slightly scrunch the paper and lay it flat on to the wall, scrunch it again slightly while it is on the surface and then lift it away cleanly.

3 Finally, scrunch the paper into a ball and dab to remove any large blobs and even up the surface pattern.

LEFT: The subtle decorative effect of frottage helps to freshen up a plain expanse of wall in a hallway.

USING PLASTIC

Using plastic for frottage gives a slightly different effect from paper. Instead of removing much of the paint, it will just make a print within it on the surface.

1 Mix 50 per cent wallpaper paste with 50 per cent emulsion (latex) in a paint kettle (pot). Brush on to the wall in a large area of about 3,000 sq cm/3 sq ft.

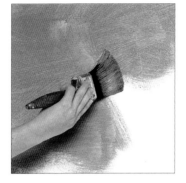

2 Take the plastic bag and scrunch it slightly before applying it to the surface. Once you have placed it against the surface, scrunch it again slightly and then lift it away cleanly.

3 Scrunch the plastic into a ball to remove any excess blobs and soften the overall effect.

FROTTAGE

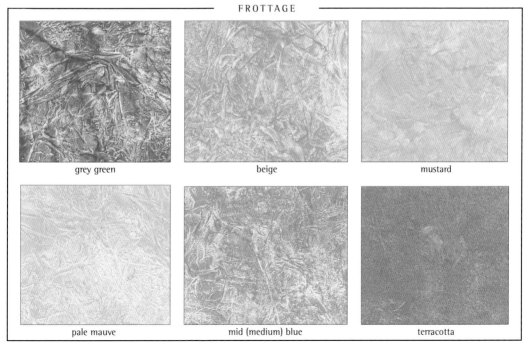

| grey green | beige | mustard |
| pale mauve | mid (medium) blue | terracotta |

SPATTERING

Spattering is produced by layering small dots of different coloured paint. It is an incredibly simple technique when applied to a flat surface, as the consistency of the paint mixture is not crucial to the final effect. If you are spattering an upright surface, however, consistency is a key element because if the paint is too thin it will simply drip down. Test the paint mixture beforehand to prevent any mistakes, which are almost impossible to correct and may result in having to start again. The basic technique of spattering is to load a paintbrush with paint and then knock this against another to launch small dots and spatters of paint onto the surface, moving the position constantly to control the distribution.

The colour of the base coat is important as this will probably remain the overall dominant colour since the spattering itself is a purely decorative rather than a covering effect. You can use a number of different colours to spatter, but simple colour combinations to try are sage over jade green, navy over lilac, mustard over terracotta, cream over camel, mauve over purple and lime green over turquoise.

1 Apply the first coat of base coat of emulsion (latex) paint.

2 Once this is dry, add a second coat of the base coat for a solid finish.

3 Mix the second colour with about 25 per cent water in a paint kettle (pot) until it is thin and creamy. Take an artist's brush and dip it into the mixture. Scrape off excess paint on to the side of the container and flick the bristles to create large dots.

4 Once the second colour is dry, take a third colour and mix with 25 per cent water in a paint kettle (pot) until it has a creamy consistency. Again, take the artist's brush, dip it into the paint, and scrape the excess on to the side of the kettle (pot). Create dots on the surface by tapping one brush on to the other.

5 Make finer dots with the third colour by flicking the bristles with your index finger.

RIGHT: This wall is spattered with a mixture of slightly diluted white and yellow emulsion paint over a navy blue base coat.

SPATTERING

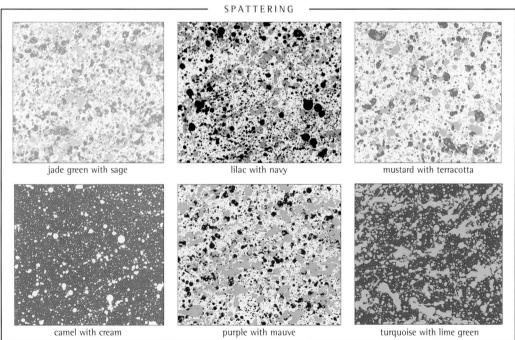

jade green with sage

lilac with navy

mustard with terracotta

camel with cream

purple with mauve

turquoise with lime green

DISTRESSING

Distressing is a way of ageing paint to create chips and scratches that would occur naturally on a painted piece of furniture over a matter of time. The two mediums used here are wax and petroleum jelly. These both create a barrier between the surface and the paint, so once the paint is dry it can be lifted away in certain areas where the medium has been applied. Therefore the careful placing of either wax or petroleum jelly is the key to the success of this technique. Concentrate on areas that would receive more wear and tear, such as edges and corners and around handles; this way the effect will look more natural. Using this technique through layers of different colours creates a more intense distressed effect. Water-based paints must be used, but you will need to varnish the surface for durability.

USING WAX

The easiest way to apply wax to distress a piece of furniture is to use a candle, as you can manipulate it across the edges and into corners. If you are applying two or more layers of paint you will need to wax and rub after each one. Once you have mastered the technique, however, it is a very inexpensive way to age new looking furniture.

Distressing one layer using wax

1 Rub with a candle over the surface in the direction of the grain. Even if the surface is not wooden, rub in a lengthways direction over a suitable coloured base coat. Concentrate on the edges where more wear would occur naturally.

You will need
◆ candle
◆ emulsion (latex) paint
◆ household paintbrush
◆ paint scraper
◆ fine-grade sandpaper
◆ varnish

2 Paint over the whole surface with a thin layer of emulsion (latex) paint and leave it to dry thoroughly.

3 Use a paint scraper to remove the paint. The paint will be removed very easily in the areas where the wax was applied as it acts as a barrier and stops the paint adhering to the surface beneath. If there is any residual wax left, remove it using fine-grade sandpaper before varnishing.

Distressing two layers using wax

1 If you wish to paint on another layer of colour, first rub over the surface again with a candle in the same direction as in the previous technique. Again concentrate on the edges. Apply the wax quite heavily, as you will need to remove more paint from the second layer to expose areas of both the first coat of paint and the original base coat or wood.

2 Paint over the whole surface with emulsion (latex) paint in a contrasting colour and then leave to dry thoroughly.

3 Again, use a paint scraper to remove the wax and reveal both the first coat and the base coat. Use sandpaper to remove any remaining wax. Varnish to protect the surface.

DISTRESSING WITH WAX

cornflower blue over wood

mauve over wood

terracotta over wood

purple over green over wood

pale yellow over burnt orange over wood

orange over blue over wood

USING PETROLEUM JELLY

Distressing with petroleum jelly produces a far more dramatic effect than using wax. The blobs of petroleum jelly used to create a barrier are bulkier and create tears in the paint that look far less scratchy than with wax. This is a good technique to use for the first layer of distressing, followed by a wax layer on top.

You will need
◆ petroleum jelly
◆ small paintbrush
◆ emulsion (latex) paint
◆ household paintbrush
◆ paint scraper
◆ soapy water
◆ varnish

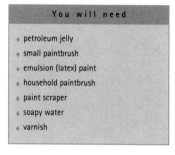

1 Using a small brush, load it with petroleum jelly and apply blobs in an elongated motion in the direction of the grain of wood over a suitably coloured base coat. Even if the surface is not wooden, rub in a lengthways direction. You can apply quite a lot of petroleum jelly but try and keep it in long blobs.

2 Carefully paint over this, ensuring that the petroleum jelly is not dragged too much as it will move under the paintbrush.

3 Once thoroughly dry, use a paint scraper to remove the blobs as these acted as a barrier between the top coat and the base coat.

4 Wash down with soapy water, as the paint that is sitting on top of the petroleum jelly will not actually dry and you will not be able to totally remove the petroleum jelly surface using the scraper.

5 Once dry, rub over with a wax candle and then paint as before. (You could use another layer of petroleum jelly, following the same procedure as for the first layer, but the finished effect would not look as subtle.)

6 When the paint is dry remove with a paint scraper. Wipe down to remove all the flakes and then varnish to protect the surface.

RIGHT: Give an old junk table a lift by applying a light blue distressed paint effect to the wood.

DISTRESSING WITH PETROLEUM JELLY

blue over yellow over wood

mauve over blue over wood

green over blue over wood

orange over yellow over wood

purple over red over wood

blue over burnt orange over wood

AGEING AND ANTIQUING

These two techniques are basically a way of eliminating the too perfect and too new look from a newly made piece of furniture. Some of the effects are more dramatic than others, some are more suitable for painted surfaces and others for wood, and sometimes the use of two effects together can achieve a successful finish. Practise on an area that is not normally visible before starting the whole piece.

Generally, ageing adds a distressed appearance to the surface while antiquing is a more delicate and refined approach, which is perhaps better suited to small decorative accessories, such as picture frames.

AGEING

These three effects are all suitable for a painted surface. You can combine them to give a more authentic aged look to a new piece of painted furniture, but be careful not to overdo the effect.

You will need

- burnt umber artists' oil colour paint
- white spirit (turpentine)
- paint kettle (pot)
- fine artist's brush
- household paintbrush

Applying age spots

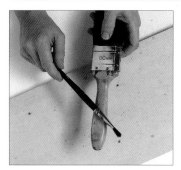

1 Mix burnt umber artists' oil colour paint with white spirit (turpentine) into a thin wash in a paint kettle (pot). Spatter lightly on the surface of the area with a brush, slightly dotting the surface.

2 While the spattered dots are wet, take a dry brush and brush in one direction. This technique will add random-shaped age spots to the surface.

For a heavy aged look

You will need

- heat gun stripper
- knife
- wire (steel) wool

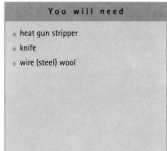

1 Remove random strips of paint from the surface of the piece of furniture with a heat gun stripper and a knife.

2 When you have finished stripping off the slivers of paint, smooth off with wire (steel) wool to slightly age the remaining paintwork.

For a lighter chipped look

1 Run a paint scraper across the newly painted surface. This will remove small chunks of paintwork.

2 Soften the effect with fine-grade sandpaper, giving more attention to the edges. Then wipe down with a damp cloth and, when dry, varnish to protect the surface.

RIGHT: You can give a very plain looking mirror an attractive rustic look by applying a heavy aged surface to it. By removing slivers of paint from the top layer of paint, the appearance of the frame is instantly transformed.

ANTIQUING

Here are three different effects that give an older look without making the surface appear too distressed. They can be done on newly painted surfaces for a subtle finish.

Applying tinted varnish

1 Apply a tinted varnish over the painted surface. These are available in various ranges of tinted colours. If you are applying the varnish to unpainted wood choose one that will complement it. For instance, use antique pine for a newly made piece of pine furniture.

2 While wet, wipe away the excess. The more you wipe away, the less old the piece will look. To remove more of the varnish, dampen the cloth with white spirit (turpentine) if oil based, or water if acrylic.

Applying button polish (shellac)

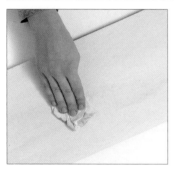

1 Rub on button polish (shellac) using a soft cloth. Ensure that the whole surface is covered.

2 While wet wipe off the excess to even out the effect.

OPPOSITE: The tinted varnish used to decorate this frame gives it an air of aged distinction. Use this method to soften the harsh appearance of a brand new wooden frame, or apply it to an old frame that needs a new treatment.

Applying a tinted wash

You will need

◆ burnt umber artists' oil colour paint
◆ white spirit (turpentine)
◆ paint kettle (pot)
◆ household paintbrush

1 Mix a little burnt umber artists' oil colour paint with white spirit (turpentine) in a paint kettle (pot) until you have a very thin wash. Brush on to the surface of the piece of furniture.

2 While wet, wipe off the excess to leave a slightly stained look. To remove the wash, dampen the cloth with white spirit (turpentine). Varnish the surface when dry to protect it.

WOOD WASHING (WOOD STAINING)

Wood washing (wood staining) actually stains wood with a colour, so that the beauty of the grain shows through and is enhanced by the colour. The technique can only be used on totally bare, stripped wood once all traces of varnish, wax or previous paint have been completely removed.

Depending on the product used, the surface may or may not need varnishing, so make sure you read the manufacturer's information on the container. Usually a matt (flat) finish looks appropriate for this technique.

Colours that often work well include yellow ochre, blue, Indian red, violet, cream and pale green.

Using a specialist (specialty) wood wash (wood stain)

You will need

- specialist (specialty) wood wash (wood stain)
- paint kettle (pot)
- household paintbrush
- cloth

1 Pour the pre-mixed wash into a paint kettle (pot). Then brush the wash (stain) evenly on the wood in the direction of the grain.

2 While wet, wipe off the excess with a cloth. This will even the effect and expose slightly more of the grain. Then, leave to dry before varnishing if required.

Using satinwood paint

You will need

- satinwood paint
- white spirit (turpentine)
- paint kettle (pot)
- household paintbrush
- cloth

1 Dilute the satinwood paint with 50 per cent white spirit (turpentine) in a paint kettle (pot). Brush the mixture on to the wood in the direction of the grain.

2 While wet, wipe down with a cloth to remove the excess and even the effect. Leave the surface to dry before varnishing if required.

Using artists' oil colour paint

1 Dilute a small blob of artists' oil colour paint with white spirit (turpentine) in a paint kettle (pot) to make a thin wash. You only need to use a small amount of colour, as the pigment is intensely strong. Brush the mixture on to the wood in the direction of the grain.

2 While wet, remove the excess with a cloth to expose a little more of the grain and even the effect. Leave to dry before varnishing if required.

ABOVE: A pale blue wood wash (stain) gives this door a nautical appearance.

WOOD WASHES (STAINS)

yellow ochre

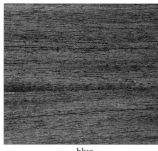

blue

Indian red

violet

cream

pale green

BASKET WEAVE

This is almost a controlled version of colourwashing in which you apply the paint in an overlapping, interlocking basket weave motion to create an overall pattern within the wet paint. The effect on a wall should be quite loose rather than precise, so that you quickly cover a large area. The basic technique involves brushing on the wash in wide columns, then taking a wide brush, starting at the top and pulling down in alternating strokes creating a criss-cross pattern down the length of the wall.

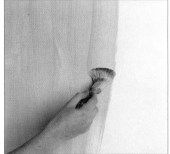

1 Mix 50 per cent emulsion (latex) paint with 50 per cent wallpaper paste (premixed to a thin solution) in a paint kettle (pot). Brush the mixture on the wall in a wide section, totally covering from the top to the bottom.

2 Working down in columns, alternate the angle of the brush from left to right in short strokes.

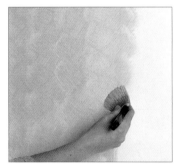

3 Continue up to the edge of each section as you go.

4 Add more paint mixture, again in a long column, slightly overlapping the previous section.

5 Redo the column that has been overlapped, using the same movement of the brush.

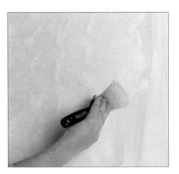

6 Continue until the wall is evenly covered with the effect.

RIGHT: Overlapping textured brushstrokes are applied to this wall to leave a basket weave effect. Pale sage-green paint is used over a base coat of white, which gives a subtle background colour.

BASKET WEAVE

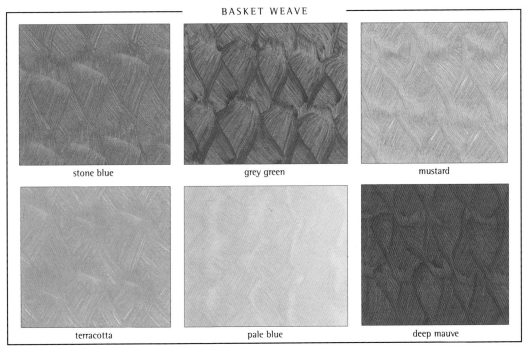

stone blue	grey green	mustard
terracotta	pale blue	deep mauve

CRACKLE GLAZE

This technique reproduces the effect of old, crackled paint, but it can only work if you use a special crackle-glaze medium. A base coat is painted first, and when dry, a layer of crackle glaze is applied. This is followed by a top coat of paint, which will not be able to grip the base coat while drying and subsequently will shrink and crack to produce a crackled effect.

You can achieve some striking colour combinations with this technique; bear in mind that the more the top coat contrasts with the base coat the more dramatic the effect will be. The size of the cracks can usually be made larger with a thicker coat of the crackle medium or by varying the thickness of the top coat of paint, depending on the product. Try a test patch beforehand.

The method of use for crackle-glaze mediums varies, so make sure you carefully follow the manufacturer's instructions. The method outlined here is a general guide.

You will need

- emulsion (latex) paint in two colours
- household paintbrush
- crackle-glaze medium

1 Apply one coat of the base colour and leave to dry thoroughly.

2 Apply a second coat of base colour and leave to dry again.

3 Apply a good solid coat of crackle-glaze medium. The timing for applying the various coats will vary according to the manufacturer, so follow the instructions given on the container.

4 Apply the top coat. Generally, the thicker the top coat of paint, the larger the cracks in the final effect. Make sure the top coat contrasts greatly with the one underneath so that the cracks are obvious. Do not overbrush when applying the top coat, as the effect happens quite quickly and you could spoil it.

CRACKLE GLAZE

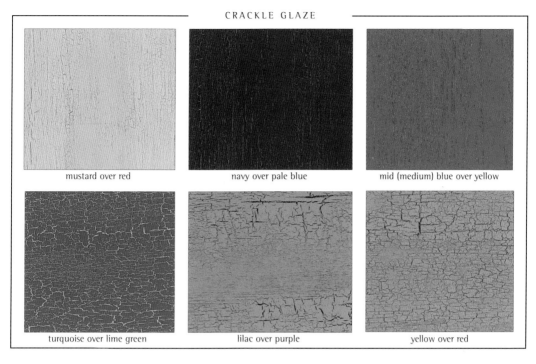

mustard over red

navy over pale blue

mid (medium) blue over yellow

turquoise over lime green

lilac over purple

yellow over red

RIGHT: This plant pot is given a crackle glaze treatment in pale blue and cream and finished with a thin border, drawn with a fine artist's brush to highlight the shape of the container.

LACQUERING

Lacquering creates a totally smooth, flat and highly polished paint finish that reflects great depth of colour. The traditional method of lacquering, as perfected by generations of Asian craftsmen, is very time consuming and consists of applying at least 16 layers of paint. The steps below describe a simulated version, though this still relies on creating a totally smooth finish using rich colours finished with a high gloss varnish. Aerosol spray paints are used for the last layers because they will create the smoothest surface possible.

This technique is still quite time consuming and it is probably wise to attempt smaller objects if you are looking for quick results. Colours that work well in a lacquered finish are turquoise, gold, red, black, deep yellow and teal green.

1 Sand the surface thoroughly until totally smooth. Then wipe clean the surface, making sure that it is completely free of dust.

2 Apply a base coat of high gloss paint and leave to dry thoroughly.

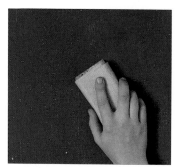

3 Sand the surface again to ensure total smoothness.

4 Apply a second base coat. Leave to dry thoroughly.

5 Spray on a gloss enamel in the same colour as the base coat. Again, leave to dry thoroughly.

6 Spray a gloss varnish over the surface to protect it and provide a final finish.

LACQUERING

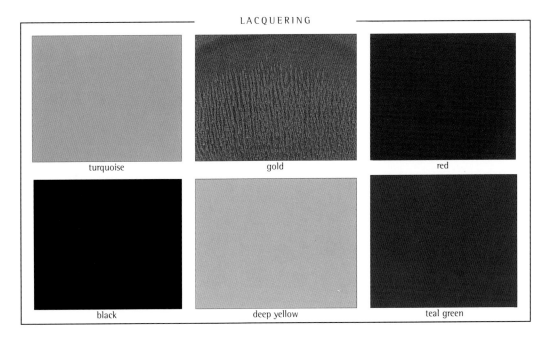

turquoise

gold

red

black

deep yellow

teal green

RIGHT: A smooth lacquered surface emphasizes the shape of this mirror sconce. Red enamel spray paint is used over a claret base coat of high gloss paint. The lacquering is protected with spray gloss varnish.

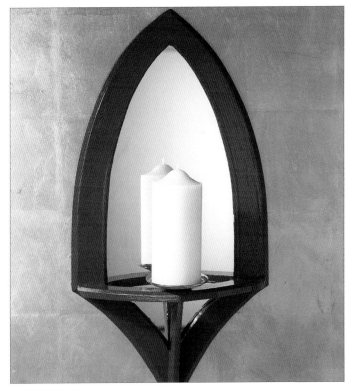

GILDING

Gilding is an attractive finish that enhances and adds a touch of luxury to furniture or smaller items and home accessories. The technique consists of placing a thin layer of gold leaf over a base coat, then burnishing and polishing it to a gloss or sheen finish. Size is used to help the gold leaf adhere, prepared by pouncing or dusting talc on to the surface first. In small areas where the gilding is rubbed away the colour of the base coat shows through and adds depth to the finished effect.

The materials needed for gilding are readily available at craft shops. As real gold leaf is expensive, you may prefer to use Dutch Metal, particularly if you are a beginner to this technique. This is an alloy that gives a similar effect, but it can become tarnished in time, so you will need to varnish it.

You will need

- paintbrushes
- acrylic primer
- grey lacquer undercoat
- dark green lacquer paint
- soft cloths or rags
- talc
- string
- water-based gilder's size
- gold leaf or Dutch Metal
- gilder's pad
- gilder's knife or sharp craft knife
- gilder's tip
- petroleum jelly
- cotton wool balls (cotton balls)
- burnishing brush or soft cloth
- wire (steel) wool
- methylated spirits (methyl alcohol)
- wadding (batting)
- liquid polish

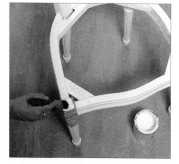

1 Prime the wood to be gilded with acrylic primer and leave to dry for a couple of hours or so.

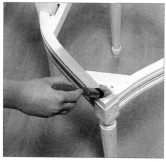

2 Paint on a coat of grey lacquer undercoat and leave to dry for at least four hours.

3 Paint on one or two coats of dark green lacquer paint and leave each coat to dry for at least six to eight hours, or overnight if possible.

4 Fill a cloth or rag with talc and close it up with string to make a pounce bag. Pounce or dust the areas to be gilded by dabbing the bag on the surface to give a thin sprinkling. Brush off any excess talc.

LEFT: Gilded plant pots make very attractive bases for colourful fresh or dried flower arrangements.

5 Paint a thin, even coat of water-based gilder's size on to the areas to be gilded and leave for 20–30 minutes, until the size becomes clear and tacky.

6 Blow a sheet of gold leaf on to a gilder's pad, cutting it into smaller pieces with a gilder's knife if required. Brush petroleum jelly on to the inside of your forearm and lightly brush the gilder's tip over the petroleum jelly. Then use the tip to pick up the leaf.

7 Lay the leaf on the sized area and gently press into place with cotton balls. Continue until the whole sized area is covered with gold leaf. Burnish with a burnishing brush or soft cloth to remove the excess leaf.

BELOW: Gilding has been used here to add decorative details to a Louis XIV chair.

8 Dip some wire (steel) wool into a little methylated spirits (methyl alcohol) and rub gently on the areas of detail to remove tiny amounts of the leaf.

9 Cover some wadding (batting) with a clean rag, leaving an opening at the top. Add a few drips of polish to soak the wadding (batting), close up and rub over the gilded areas.

STAINED GLASS

Everyone loves the bright jewel colours of stained glass, and it is an easy matter to decorate ordinary household glass containers by painting freehand with special glass paints. Choose colours and motifs to match your china or curtains, or experiment with messages and make up your own patterns. Another interesting technique is to replicate the look of etched glass, relying on the frosted design to give a subtle surface effect. Glass paints and etching paste are available at craft shops.

ETCHING GLASS

Create the pattern or motifs you require by masking the glass with self-adhesive vinyl. The etching paste (cream), will eat the surface of the glass that is not protected by vinyl to produce a frosted effect.

You will need
◆ self-adhesive vinyl
◆ scissors
◆ rubber gloves for protection
◆ etching paste (cream)
◆ 2.5cm/1in flat paintbrush
◆ clean cotton rag

1 Draw your designs on self-adhesive vinyl and cut out. Decide where you want to position them on the glass, then remove the backing paper from the vinyl and stick them down.

2 Wearing rubber gloves for protection, paint the etching paste (cream) evenly over the glass with a paintbrush. Make sure you do not spread it too thinly, or you will find the effect quite faint. Leave to dry for three minutes.

3 Wearing rubber gloves, wash the paste (cream) off under a running tap. Wipe off any residue and rinse. Peel off the shapes, and wash the glass again. Dry the glass with a clean cotton rag.

LEFT: Painted glass picture frames.

PAINTED GLASS

Use simple plain glass objects to decorate and add as much decoration and colour as you like.

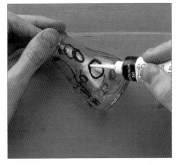

1 Start by drawing a few loose circles on to the pots with black contour relief paint (leading).

2 When the lines are completely dry, colour in the background using the glass paint.

3 Fill in the circles with a different coloured paint or use a variety of different colours.

4 Apply dots of black contour paint (leading) over the background colour to add texture.

5 When completely dry, paint squares over the circles using the gold contour relief paint (leading).

6 Leave the pots to dry for at least 4 hours, then paint with clear varnish.

RIGHT: There are endless plain glass items you can decorate. Simple designs of circles and squares can look stunning outlined in black paint.

PATTERNED
EFFECTS

There are many ways of applying pattern as a
decoration, whether freehand or using a template.
With stencilling and stamping you can add an
individual touch to your schemes by choosing
designs from a wealth that are available
commercially or by drawing, cutting and using your
own stencils and stamps. Classic lines and stripes
never seem to go out of fashion, and grid patterns
are a fun way of combining colours.

STENCILLING

Stencilling is one of the most popular of paint effects, and with good reason – the decorative possibilities are endless. It is an ideal way to create an interesting border or all-over pattern using motifs that relate to the theme of your room. Stencilling also enables you to co-ordinate furnishings and accessories by picking out details in similar or contrasting colours. Or you can use the patterns and colours of your stencilling as a starting point for the style and colours of your home. Try using rich colour groupings such as a combination of camel, deep red and purple.

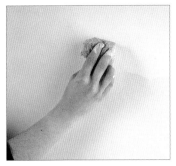

1 Using a large household sponge, rub your first colour of emulsion (latex) paint over the wall. Leave to dry. Repeat using a second colour to cover the base.

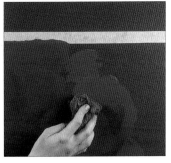

2 Using a ruler and spirit level (level), draw a line at dado (chair) height and place a line of masking tape above it. Sponge your third colour below this.

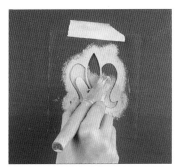

3 Trace the heraldic templates from the back of the book and cut stencils from stencil card (card stock) or acetate. Secure the rose stencil above the dividing line and stencil in your third colour with a stencil brush. When dry, position the fleur-de-lis stencil next to the first and paint in the colour of the base coat. Alternate the stencils around the room to make a border.

4 Make some highlighting stencils using the same templates. Place them over the painted motifs and, with a stencil brush, add highlights in the base colour to the first stencil and highlights in the third colour to the second stencil.

RIGHT: Richly coloured walls and heraldic motifs are stencilled in the same deep tones to lend an atmosphere of luxury.

5 Flip the stencils over and position as mirror images below the original motifs. Stencil the roses in the base colour and the fleur-de-lis in the third colour.

BELOW: Create a medieval dining room with these decorative stencils and add gilt accessories, heavy fabrics and a profusion of candles to complete the look.

6 Add highlights as before, using base colour on the fleurs-de-lis and the third colour on the roses.

7 Using a fine lining brush and the base colour paint, paint a narrow line where the two different colours on the wall meet. If you do not have the confidence to do this freehand, position two rows of masking tape on the wall, leaving a small gap in between. When the line of paint is dry, carefully remove the masking tape.

STAMPING

Stamping is another way of creating your own motifs to decorate your home. It is easy and inexpensive to cut out shapes in relief from high-density sponge and to use them to apply paint. However, you can also achieve quite sophisticated effects with this simple technique, and the steps below describe how to add a special touch to a room by stamping panels with gold leaf. This effect is achieved by stamping the wall with gold size first and then rubbing on gold leaf, which will adhere to the tacky surface. Dutch Metal is used because it is much less expensive than real gold, but it produces a stunning effect when combined with deep colours.

You will need

- card (card stock)
- ruler
- scissors
- pencil
- high-density sponge
- craft knife
- emulsion (latex) paint in jade green and purple
- household sponge
- plumb line
- tape measure
- small paint roller
- gold size
- Dutch Metal
- soft brush

1 Cut out a piece of card (card stock) measuring 10cm/4in x 10cm/4in. To make a template for wall panels, draw a freehand arc from the centre top of the card to the bottom corner.

2 Fold the card (card stock) in half down the centre and cut out both sides to make a single symmetrical Gothic arch shape.

3 Trace the design from the back of the book and make a paper pattern. Transfer the design on to a piece of high-density sponge. Using a craft knife, cut away the excess sponge from around the flower shape.

4 Apply jade green emulsion (latex) paint on to the wall using a sponge and working in a circular motion. Allow the paint to dry.

5 Using a plumb line as a guide, and beginning 23cm/9in from a corner, mark a vertical line up the wall to a height of 1.8m/6ft.

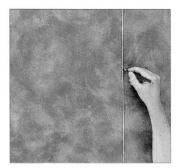

6 Measure across the wall and use the plumb line to draw vertical lines every 60cm/2ft.

7 Measure out 15cm/6in each side of each vertical line and draw two more vertical lines to mark the edges of the panels on the wall.

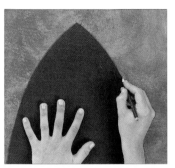

8 Place the point of the card (card stock) template at the centre top point of each panel and draw in the curves.

9 Load the stamp with gold size and print each panel, beginning with the centre top and working down.

10 When the size is tacky, apply Dutch gold leaf by rubbing over the backing paper with a soft brush.

11 Once the panel is complete, use a soft brush to remove any excess gold leaf.

12 Using the centre of the stamp, fill in the spaces between the gold motifs with purple emulsion (latex) paint.

RIGHT: Gold stamps add an air of opulence to this dining room setting.

LINING

This is a clever way of creating highly decorative and structured objects, emphasizing the basic shape of a piece or outlining areas. It can be done over any previously paint-effected surface, wood or flat colour. For maximum impact, the colours used should contrast or relate closely to the original base coats.

There are various ways of achieving fine lines. The easiest is to use masking tape, and even beginners can produce successful painted lines using this method. Specialist (specialty) brushes and professional signwriters' lining brushes with long bristles are best since they hold a great deal of paint and hold a good line, though you need a steady hand and a lot of practice. Swordliners (liners) hold a good amount of paint and give a fine line, but you must keep the pressure constant, or the line's thickness will vary.

1 Apply a base coat. Ensure that two coats are applied as the surface must be completely solid colour.

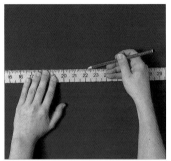

2 Draw a line using a pencil and ruler.

3 Mask this off on both sides, creating a fine but even line. Make sure that the masking tape is flat to the surface. Paint in the line in the second colour.

4 Remove the masking tape, pulling away from the line slowly.

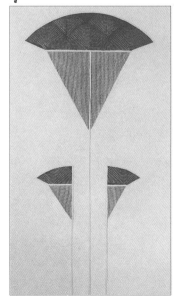

RIGHT: A coach line, such as used for decorating cars, creates an even finer line if you would prefer not to handle a brush.

STRIPES

Stripes are a classic design for decorating schemes. They are extremely versatile, as you can vary their width for any number of effects. If you are aiming for a symmetrical, formal look it is important to measure out the available space accurately first so that you can be sure the stripes will fit. It is helpful to draw out the design on a small scale on a piece of paper to work out the correct balance to scale.

BELOW: *Wide stripes look smart in a modern kitchen.*

1 Paint the walls, using a paint roller and tray. Mark the centre of the most important wall, below the picture rail (if you have one), with a pencil. Make marks 7.5cm/3in on either side of this, then every 15cm/6in. Continue around the room until the marks meet at the least noticeable corner.

2 Hang a short length of plumb line from one of the marks, and mark with a dot where it rests. Then, hang the plumb line from this dot and mark where it rests. Continue down the wall. Repeat for each mark below the picture rail.

3 Starting in the centre of the wall, place strips of masking tape on either side of the marked row of dots to give a 15cm/6in wide stripe. Repeat for the other rows of dots.

4 Dilute some of the second colour paint with about 25 per cent water and 25 per cent acrylic scumble. Brush on to a section of the first stripe. Complete each stripe in two or three stages, depending on the height of the room, blending the joins (seams) to achieve an even result.

5 Dab the wet paint lightly with a cloth to smooth out the brushmarks. Complete all the stripes, peel off the masking tape and leave the paint to dry.

6 From a piece of cardboard cut a triangle with a 15cm/6in base and measuring 10cm/4in from base to tip. Use this to mark the centre of each stripe.

BELOW: The formality of the stripes is softened by the use of light colours.

7 Working on one strip at a time, place strips of masking tape between the top corners of the stripe and the marked dot. Brush on the second colour paint, then dab the stockinette (nylon stocking) cloth over the wet paint as before. Leave to dry and repeat for all stripes.

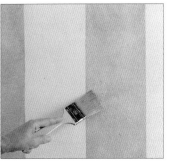

8 Dilute some of the second colour paint with 20 parts water. Brush over the wall in all directions to give a hint of colour to the first colour stripes.

9 Add a little paint to the remaining diluted mixture to strengthen the colour. Using a paint guard or strip of card to protect the painted wall, brush the paint on to the picture rail.

TARTAN (PLAID)

Painting a tartan (plaid) surface is a fun technique to create an interesting patterned fabric effect. By overlapping different coloured grids of colour, using varying widths of lines, endless combinations can be achieved. Replicating a colour scheme from an actual piece of checked or tartan (plaid) fabric, for instance on a cushion or a throw, can save a lot of trial and error and can be a good way of continuing a theme in a room scheme. When planning the technique and drawing the grid, take the width of bands into account. If they are too close the whole effect will look busy, but if too spaced they will look weak.

Traditional tartan (plaid) colours work well, as do the following: a jade base with mid (medium) greens; a navy base with pale blue and pale yellow; a red base with dark green and yellow; a grey base with lilac and white; a pale yellow base with pale blue and navy; or a grey-green base with mint green and dark red.

1 Apply the base coat of paint. Make sure the colour is completely solid – two coats may be needed.

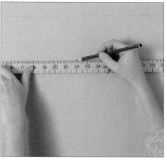

2 Draw on the grid, using a pencil, plumb line and ruler. Bear in mind the width of the paint roller you are going to use while drawing the grid.

3 Apply the second colour on to the roller and roller down one side of the drawn lines. Leave to dry.

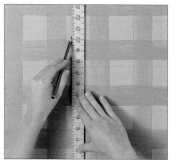

4 Draw the grid for the fine lines using a ruler and pencil.

5 Mix the third colour with a little water until a thin cream. Add the fine line in one direction using a lining brush. Leave to dry.

6 Complete the pattern by adding in the cross strokes.

RIGHT: If you do not want to decorate a whole wall, simply add a couple of bands of tartan (plaid) at dado (chair) rail height, beneath the level of the window.

TARTAN (PLAID)

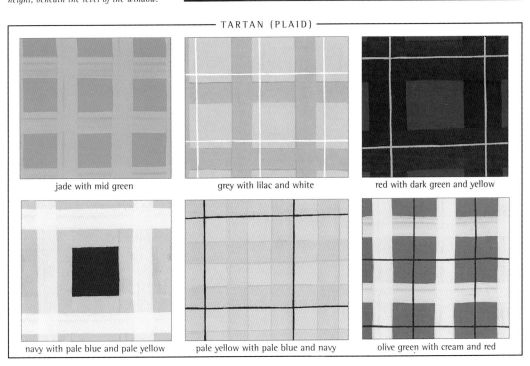

| jade with mid green | grey with lilac and white | red with dark green and yellow |
| navy with pale blue and pale yellow | pale yellow with pale blue and navy | olive green with cream and red |

PRINTED TILES

This is an inexpensive and clever way to create a tiled effect with simple painted squares. Fine tape separates the tiles and is removed when the effect is finished to give the illusion of grouting. Leave some of the squares plain, but add extra effects to others by sponging them or dabbing them with a stockinette (nylon stocking) cloth. Experiment with different colours to create your own design, or leave some of the squares white as a contrast. You could also experiment with mosaic patterns by measuring and masking much smaller squares with fine line tape before applying the second colour.

1 Paint the wall that you are using for this effect in white, using a paint roller for an even texture. Decide on the width of your tiled panel. Mark the wall 45cm/18in above your work surface and in the centre of the width measurement.

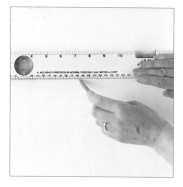

2 Draw a horizontal line at this height, using a spirit level (level) to make sure that it is straight. Place a strip of masking tape above this line.

3 Mark dots along the tape at 15cm/6in intervals on either side of the centre mark. Use the spirit level (level) to draw vertical lines down the wall. Mark dots along the vertical lines at 15cm/6in intervals and connect them to draw horizontal lines.

LEFT AND RIGHT: Tiles are most commonly used in kitchens and bathrooms – this paint effect creates the same look, but without all the hard work!

4 Place fine masking tape over the lines in both directions. Smooth the tape into place with your fingers, pressing it down well to ensure that as little paint as possible will be able to seep underneath it.

5 Place low-tack masking tape around one square. Pour the second colour paint into the paint tray and add 25 per cent water. Apply an even coat of paint to the roller, then roll it over the square. Repeat for all the plain squares.

6 Mask off a square to be sponged. Dampen the sponge, dip it into the second colour paint and dab the excess on to kitchen paper (paper towels). Sponge the paint on to the square. Repeat for all of the sponged squares.

7 Mask off a square to be dabbed with the stockinette (nylon stocking) cloth. Apply the paint with a brush, then use the cloth to blend it. Repeat for all the squares you want to have this effect.

8 Remove all the tape and clean off the pencil marks.

FREEHAND

A simple design painted freehand is an easy way to decorate small surfaces. Sometimes beginners have trouble deciding what to paint, so here is an idea to follow for a wooden table with a drawer. It is painted in harmonizing colours with a simple leaf motif. If the surface you are painting is new, sand the wood first with fine-grade sandpaper and paint with a coat of primer. You could also paint a tray or some wooden boxes to match, or use the idea as a launching pad for some bright, adventurous colours and abstract designs.

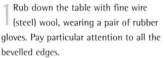

1 Rub down the table with fine wire (steel) wool, wearing a pair of rubber gloves. Pay particular attention to all the bevelled edges.

2 Using dark yellow emulsion (latex) paint, paint the mouldings, if there are any, around the edge of the table.

3 Paint the rest of the table with two coats of grey-green emulsion (latex), allowing the paint to dry between coats.

4 Wearing rubber gloves once again, rub down the entire surface with wire (steel) wool.

5 Mix 50 parts white emulsion (latex) paint with 50 parts scumble. Apply sparsely to the grey-green areas with a dry brush, using light diagonal strokes and varying the angle of the brush to give an even coverage.

OPPOSITE: This simple little design transforms a plain table into a decorative piece of furniture.

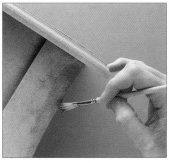

6 Mix 50 parts dark yellow emulsion (latex) paint with 50 parts scumble. Paint this over the mouldings.

7 Apply light dabs of mid (medium) green paint to the parts that would receive the most wear – the top corners of the legs and underneath. Leave to dry, then rub back with wire (steel) wool.

8 Paint a scrolling leaf design around the edge of the drawer front in pale green using a fine artbrush. Pick out the stalks and leaf veins with fine brushstrokes in mid green.

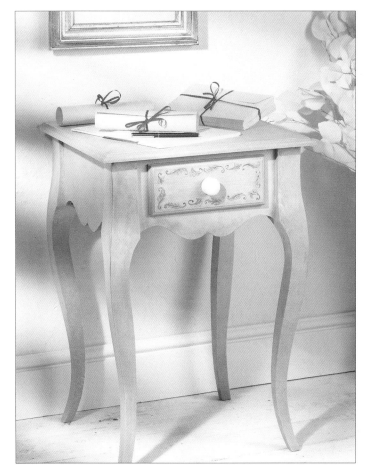

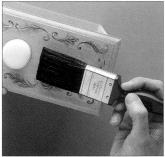

9 Still using the fine artbrush, add white and yellow highlights to the leaf design.

10 Seal the table with a coat of acrylic varnish for protection.

FAUX
FINISHES

Techniques that reproduce the look of a particular

surface or material are great fun and satisfying to

paint. The following pages describe a number of

wood and stone finishes for which artists' oil

colours are used, as the lengthy drying times allow

more time to work into the effect, and the colours

are intense and translucent. Enamel paints are used

for metal effects and emulsion (latex) paints for

animal prints and trompe l'oeil decorations.

BIRDSEYE MAPLE

Birdseye maple has an attractive close grain. The wood is often used for parquet flooring as well as for furniture and was popular in the 1930s. This technique is useful if you wish to re-create the look of that era. Birdseye maple has a slightly yellowish tinge, so a pale yellow paint is used for the base coat for this effect. One of the features of the patterning of maple grain is its "eyes" and these are easy to make by simply using your fingertips. Practise on small pieces, before trying a large area, such as floorboards.

You will need

- satin or gloss finish paint in pale yellow
- artists' oil colour paint in Naples yellow and flake white
- white spirit (turpentine)
- paint kettle (pot)
- household paintbrush
- large paintbrush
- varnish

1 Apply two coats of pale yellow satin or gloss finish paint as a base coat. Leave to dry thoroughly. Mix Naples yellow artists' oil colour paint with a little flake white and white spirit (turpentine) until you have a mixture the consistency of a thick cream. Brush on.

2 Drag the glaze in one direction using the same brush as in step 1.

3 To make the pattern in the wet paint push the bristles of the brush into the glaze, coming down within columns, alternating the angles in a tight zigzag.

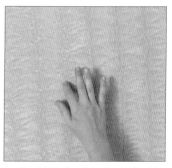

4 To add the "eyes" to the maple, dab your finger into the wet glaze around the edges of the pattern.

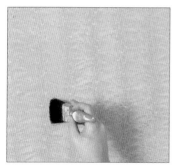

5 Leave for two hours, then soften gently using a large dry brush in a stippling motion. Varnish when dry.

RIGHT: These dishes are given a lovely birdseye maple finish. Here yellow ochre artists' oil colour paint is applied on a base coat of satin or gloss finish paint. A coat of gloss varnish protects the surface.

OAK

Perhaps nothing speaks more of a traditional style than solid oak wood furniture or panelling. Here is a way of disguising inexpensive white wood or modern pine and giving it the look of dark oak. If you are painting bare wood, remember to give it a coat of primer before starting the paint effect. This technique requires a heart grainer (graining roller) and a comb to recreate the details of the woodgrain, both of which can be bought quite easily at craft shops or specialist (specialty) decorating shops.

1 Apply two coats of beige for the base coat in either gloss or satin finish and leave to dry thoroughly.

2 Mix burnt umber artists' oil colour paint with white spirit (turpentine) in a small paint kettle (pot) until it is the consistency of thick cream. Brush on and drag in a lengthways direction.

3 Using a graduated comb, pull down on the surface, not in totally straight lines, butting one up against the other.

4 Use a heart grainer (graining roller) to start making the details of the graining. Do this by pulling the tool down gently with a slight rocking motion, to create the hearts with random spacings. Butt one line straight over the other as you go.

5 Using a fine graduated comb, comb over all the previous combing.

6 Wrap a cloth around the comb and dab on to the surface to create the angled grain, pressing into the wet paint. Then soften the overall effect using a large dry brush. Varnish when dry.

BELOW: An old junk cupboard can be picked up inexpensively and by adding an oak finish, here using burnt sienna for a warmer feel, it is instantly transformed into a beautiful piece of furniture.

MAHOGANY

This beautiful hardwood has a rich, warm colour that seems to suit most styles of home, whether traditional or modern. It was extremely popular during the Victorian era when it was complemented by deep-toned furnishings and fabrics. Mahogany is not as easy to obtain as it once was and is an expensive wood, so all the more reason to paint some for yourself. Practise on sample pieces first to get the effect right, then progress to larger furniture when you have more confidence in the technique.

BELOW: Achieve a deeper mahogany finish with a red base coat rather than dusky pink. The rich tones on this chair are produced by using burnt sienna and burnt umber artists' oil colours.

1 Apply two coats of dusky pink satin or gloss finish paint as a base coat and leave to dry. Tint a little burnt sienna artists' oil colour paint with a touch of crimson. Add white spirit (turpentine) until it reaches the consistency of thick cream. Brush it on in elongated sections.

2 Then mix burnt umber with a little white spirit (turpentine) until the mixture is the consistency of thick cream. Fill in the gaps, making elongated shapes.

3 Stipple the surface gently, using the tips of the bristles of a dry paintbrush to soften and blend the overall effect.

4 Starting at the bottom, with a 10cm/4in paintbrush held almost parallel to the surface, drag through the wet paint making elongated arcs. Use the burnt umber area as the middle section. Leave for several hours. Then, before completely dry, soften in one direction using a large dry brush. Varnish when dry.

BEECH

Beech is a light-coloured, straight-grained wood and its close patterning gives it a look of solidity. Beech has become popular in recent years for both furniture and home accessories such as trays, and mirror and picture frames. Its soft, warm colour and generally matt finish adds a quiet, but modern, tone to a room as well as helping to lighten it up. Like oak, beech is sometimes given a limed effect, so if this is what you require allow more of the base coat to show through when painting.

You will need

- satinwood paint in white
- artists' oil colour paint in Naples yellow and white
- white spirit (turpentine)
- paint kettle (pot)
- household paintbrush
- heart grainer (graining roller)
- fine graduated comb
- narrow comb
- varnish

1 Apply two coats of white satinwood paint and leave each to dry. Mix Naples yellow and artists' oil colour with a little white spirit (turpentine) until it reaches the consistency of thick cream, then brush it over the surface. Drag this in a single, lengthways direction.

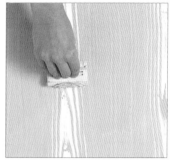

2 Use a heart grainer (graining roller) to start making the graining. Do this by pulling the tool down gently, slightly rocking it and working in several spaced lines. Do not butt the lines up together.

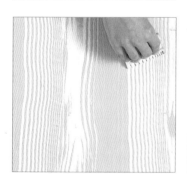

3 With a graduated comb and working in the same direction, fill in the lines between the heart graining.

4 Again, working in the same direction, soften the effect with a large dry brush. Now take a narrow comb and go over the entire surface in the same direction to add detail to the effect. Varnish when dry.

RIGHT: *A beech effect used on a table top.*

PINE

Woodgraining and wood effects can seem difficult and daunting to the beginner, but the right choice of colours and suitable base coats can be half the battle. The only specialist (specialty) tools used are a heart grainer (graining roller) and comb, which are necessary as the patterns they create cannot be imitated in any other way. Both are relatively simple to use with a little practice and create convincing effects.

Look at pieces of real wood so that you can learn to replicate the grain accurately. Pine is readily available and you can use a pine effect surface in many locations throughout your home.

You will need

- satinwood paint in pale yellow
- artists' oil colour paint in yellow ochre and burnt umber
- white spirit (turpentine)
- household paintbrush
- paint kettle (pot)
- heart grainer (graining roller)
- large paintbrush
- varnish

1 Apply two coats of pale yellow satinwood paint to the surface and leave to dry thoroughly.

2 Mix yellow ochre artists' oil colour paint with a tiny amount of burnt umber to dirty the colour slightly. Then mix with white spirit to create a thick cream, and brush over the surface.

3 Drag the brush in a lengthways direction over the wet paint to simulate planks.

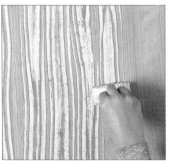

4 Following the direction of the dragging, pull the heart grainer (graining roller) down gently, rocking it as you work, to create the effect. Butt one line straight over the other.

5 Make a graduated cone shape in random areas in between the heart graining, slightly overlapping it in areas.

6 Soften the surface while wet with a large dry brush by applying only light pressure and brushing in the direction of the effect. Varnish when dry.

BELOW: Wooden floors are ever increasing in popularity and this paint technique is ideal for covering a large area very inexpensively. The chequerboard design used here adds an interesting touch to this natural-look flooring.

BURR WALNUT

Burr walnut is one of the most decorative of wood grains. It is found extensively in furniture where matching panels are used. It is even used for the dashboards of luxury motor cars and for the interior fittings of boats. It is a warm, mid-brown colour, and its graining is fun to replicate because the shapes within the wood are worked with a flowing movement. Make the burrs or "eyes" of the walnut with a piece of cloth wrapped round your index finger, so that the paint blends naturally.

You will need

- artists' oil colour paint in yellow ochre and burnt sienna
- white spirit (turpentine)
- paint kettle (pot)
- household paintbrush
- household cloth (dish cloth)
- large paintbrush
- varnish

1 Mix yellow ochre artists' oil colour paint with a little white spirit (turpentine) until you have a mixture the consistency of thick cream. Brush the mixture on in patches.

2 Then, mix burnt sienna oil colour paint with a little white spirit (turpentine) until a thick cream. Using this mixture, fill in the patches where the yellow ochre has been left.

3 Stipple the whole area with the tips of the bristles of the brush to slightly soften the paint and gently blend the colours together.

4 Fold a household cloth (dish cloth) until it is a square shape and a straight edge is achieved. Make circular ribbon shapes, gently pulling the cloth from side to side while doing this to make the pattern. Overlap the circular ribbon shapes.

5 To make the "eyes" of the burr walnut, wrap the cloth over your index finger and dab to make circular points around the ribbon shapes.

6 When nearly dry (about four hours) slightly soften with a large dry brush. Varnish when dry.

BELOW: A burr walnut effect is a suitable effect for a small treasure chest. Apply a pale yellow base coat, then paint on the effect with yellow ochre oil colour paint. This gives a lighter overall effect than burnt sienna. The edging, bands and lock are painted in gold.

MALACHITE

This green mineral is one of the most beautiful stones. It takes a high polish and is ideal for small ornaments. Malachite has circular and ribbon-like patterning and the colour within the stone ranges from pale green through viridian to a deep Prussian green. Use this effect to paint home accessories such as plain wood boxes, photograph frames and table lamps. A malachite finish is ideal for painted gifts.

You will need

- satin or gloss finish paint in jade green
- artists' oil colour paint in Prussian green and viridian green
- household paintbrush
- card (card stock) about 10cm/4in square
- fine artist's brush
- gloss varnish

1 Apply two coats of jade-green satin or gloss finish paint and leave to dry thoroughly. Apply patches of Prussian green artists' oil colour without diluting it.

3 Stipple the whole surface with the tips of the bristles of the brush to blend the edges and even the effect.

2 Then, fill in the patches where there is no Prussian green with undiluted viridian green artists' oil.

BELOW: A hexagonal box painted with a green malachite effect makes a good gift. Viridian green artists' oil colour paint is used on top of a jade green base coat.

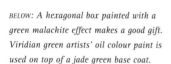

4 Hand tear a straightedge from a piece of card (card stock). Make circular ribbon shapes with it, adjusting the cardboard from side to side.

5 Using the end of an artist's brush, outline each circular shape about 1.25cm/$\frac{1}{2}$in from the actual edge. Varnish when dry.

AGATE

Agate is a type of silica rock. When cut and highly polished it reveals flowing ribbon-like patterns. These vary according to the type of agate, and their names, such as "moss" or "clouded", describe the form of patterning. Although it is seen in a wide range of colours, agate is most usually found in rich brown and ochre tones. This stone was much favoured by the Victorians for jewellery, and as decorative inlay in furniture.

1 Apply two coats of white satin or gloss finish paint as a base coat. Leave to dry thoroughly. Mix Naples yellow artists' oil colour paint with a touch of burnt umber in a paint kettle (pot) until slightly brown. Add white spirit (turpentine) until you have a mixture that is the consistency of thin cream and brush on. Then drag this in one direction.

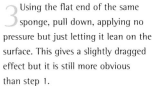

2 While it is wet gently dab over with a dry sponge in certain areas.

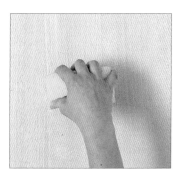

3 Using the flat end of the same sponge, pull down, applying no pressure but just letting it lean on the surface. This gives a slightly dragged effect but it is still more obvious than step 1.

4 Fold the sponge cloth and pull down in a slightly wobbly manner, making sure to drag to give a ribbon effect.

5 Soften the effect with a large dry brush. Varnish when dry.

RIGHT: An agate trug.

STONE BLOCKING

Paint these stone blocking effects in your home for a look of permanence and solidity that is usually associated with old traditional buildings and grand mansions. Two effects are described here. The first, stone blocking, replicates the slightly haphazard look of natural stone, and the second reproduces formal stone that has been carved into precise blocks.

STONE BLOCKING

The charm of this technique owes much to the mottled effect used for the pieces of stone. The various indentations of the surface of the stone take on subtle changes in colour as they become weathered. Paint highlights on to the blocks to enhance the natural look.

1 Use a large brush to apply a base coat of stone yellow emulsion (latex) paint in random sweeping strokes, leaving a mottled surface. Leave to dry thoroughly.

You will need

◆ emulsion (latex) paint in stone yellow, off-white and beige
◆ large brush
◆ card (card stock) A3 size (29 x 42cm/11½ x 16½in)
◆ pencil
◆ 2.5cm/1in paintbrush
◆ swordliner (liner)

2 Repeat step 1 using off-white emulsion (latex) paint but apply this with a dry brush, scraping off the excess and applying the paint to the surface in alternating directions, not totally covering the base coat.

3 Using card (card stock), and starting round the bottom corner, draw round with a pencil to give the outline of the stone blocks.

4 Using the off-white emulsion (latex) from step 2, add a lighter patch to the left and bottom patch of each block. Blend into the middle with a dry brush.

5 With a swordliner (liner) and beige emulsion (latex) paint, outline each block, slightly curving the corners. The edges do not have to be rigidly straight.

6 Again, with a swordliner (liner), using the off-white paint from step 2, add a rough highlighted edge to the top and right edge of each block. This can be far rougher than before, as it will stand as a highlight to give form to the stone instead of sectioning up the blocks.

RIGHT: Stone blocking in a hallway.

FORMAL STONE BLOCKING

Here the blocks of stone have been formalized so that they have precise rectangular corners like carved blocks. To ensure their regularity a grid is used as a base. Carefully painted highlighted and shadowed edges complete the effect.

1 Dip a sponge into stone yellow emulsion (latex) paint and apply to the wall in a circular motion, creating an overall mottled effect.

You will need

- sponge
- emulsion (latex) paint in stone yellow, off-white and beige
- spirit level (level)
- pencil
- paint kettle (pot)
- wallpaper paste
- 1.25cm/^{1}/$_2$in flat end paintbrush

2 Add a second coat of the stone yellow emulsion (latex) paint in patches and leave to dry.

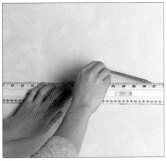

3 Using a spirit level (level), draw a grid simulating the blocks to produce an accurate grid for the stone blocking.

  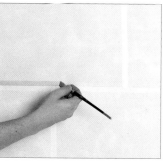

4 Mix 50 per cent off-white emulsion (latex) paint with 50 per cent wallpaper paste. Using a 1.25cm/¹/₂in flat end paintbrush, paint a stroke across the top and right hand of each block. Leave to dry.

5 Mix 50 per cent beige emulsion (latex) paint with 50 per cent wallpaper paste in a small paint kettle (pot). Use the same flat end paintbrush to paint along the bottom and left of each block, beginning each line on a mitred corner.

6 Make sure the mitred corners are painted neatly.

BELOW: The accessories and furniture in this setting perfectly complement the "church" look of the stone blocking.

GRANITE

This granite effect is great fun to paint. It allows you the pretence of living in an ancient castle with all the warmth and modern convenience that are not usually found in real buildings made of granite. If large expanses of granite wall seem too overbearing to you, however, try just painting a fire hearth.

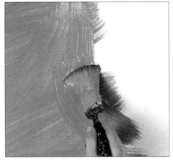

1 Mix equal parts of mid grey emulsion (latex) paint and wallpaper paste. Brush on to the surface.

2 Stipple the whole area while it is wet. Leave to dry thoroughly.

3 Take a sponge and dip into darker grey emulsion (latex). Wipe off the excess and sponge lightly over the whole surface until an even colour is achieved – the base colour should remain visible.

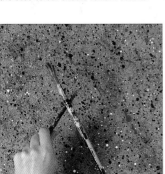

BELOW: A plant pot is given the granite treatment, in white, black and grey.

4 Mix black emulsion (latex) with water until it is the consistency of thick cream. Dip a small brush into this and wipe off the excess. Then take it over the surface, tapping the handle with another brush, to achieve a spattering effect.

5 Repeat with white emulsion (latex) paint mixed with water and with a small brush spatter over the whole surface by tapping the handle of the brush with another. Then take the mid grey base coat and spatter over the whole surface until the effect is even.

TORTOISESHELL

Real tortoiseshell actually comes from the beautiful shells of turtles and has been used for many years to make small decorative personal items such as combs, hair ornaments, needlework boxes, mirrorbacks and similar treasures. Its appearance is still admired, and plastic reproductions have taken the place of real shell. This technique uses artists' oil colours worked over a metallic enamel paint base to give depth.

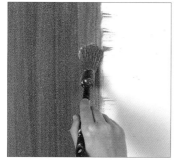

1 Apply a coat of gold enamel and leave to dry thoroughly.

2 Mix yellow ochre artists' oil colour paint and white spirit (turpentine) until it reaches the consistency of thin cream. Brush a very thin layer of the mixture over the whole surface.

3 Mix burnt sienna artists' oil colour paint with white spirit (turpentine) to make a mixture the consistency of thick cream. Paint the mixture on in dashes, working in one direction in a diagonal motion over the wet yellow.

4 Mix Naples yellow artists' oil colour paint with white spirit (turpentine) until you have a thick creamy consistency, and add dashes of it between the burnt sienna dashes.

5 Soften the paint in the same direction with a brush.

6 Mix burnt umber artists' oil colour paint with white spirit (turpentine) until a thick cream. Add small dashes to the surface. Spatter a small amount of this mixture over the top of the surface and soften with a brush, again working in one direction. Varnish when dry.

BELOW: *To make a richer tortoiseshell effect, use a red basecoat. This makes an attractive finish for a box of paints.*

LAPIS LAZULI

Lapis lazuli was favoured by the ancient Egyptians who carved it into ornaments and amulets that bore the sacred scarab beetle. Artists throughout history have ground down this stone to produce a stunning, brilliant blue pigment that formed the basis of ultramarine. This technique shows you how to paint a lapis lazuli stone effect using modern synthetic paints that closely resemble the colours of the true mineral.

You will need

- satin or gloss finish paint in mid (medium) blue
- household paintbrush
- artists' oil colour paint in ultramarine and Prussian blue
- enamel paint in silver, gold and red
- medium artist's brush
- varnish

1 Apply two coats of blue satin or gloss finish paint and leave to dry. Then apply random patches of undiluted ultramarine blue artists' oil colour.

2 Apply random patches of undiluted Prussian blue artists' oil colour paint, filling in patches where the ultramarine blue has not been put.

3 Stipple over the whole surface with the tips of the bristles of the brush to blend the colours slightly together.

4 Spatter over the whole surface by dipping an artist's brush in silver enamel paint, wiping off the excess and tapping the handle of one brush on to the handle of another over the painting.

5 Repeat step 4 with gold enamel paint, again spattering the paint over the whole surface.

6 Similarly, spatter over the whole surface using red enamel paint. Varnish when dry.

LEFT: *This amphora, bought from a garden centre, has been decorated with lapis lazuli round the base and gilding at the neck, to give it an ancient feel. The deep ultramarine base is reminiscent of the colour favoured by ancient Egyptians.*

WROUGHT IRON

Here, black and silver are carefully blended to give a realistic effect of wrought iron. The light catches and enhances the shape. The technique uses the same kind of enamel paints that are used on real wrought iron to protect it from the elements. You can create the illusion on a variety of surfaces, including wood, but make sure that you key the surface by sanding down before you start.

You will need

- sandpaper
- cardboard or tape for masking
- enamel paint in black and silver
- household paintbrush
- cloth

1 Rub down the object with sandpaper. Mask off any areas that you do not want to get paint on.

2 Apply a base coat of black enamel paint and leave it to dry thoroughly.

3 Stipple small patches of silver enamel paint over the whole surface very lightly with the tips of a brush.

4 Lightly stipple with black enamel paint in random patches.

5 Before the black paint is dry wipe over some of it with a cloth, leaving the raised areas with a more polished look.

LEFT: Wrought iron makes an unusual effect for this box. The undercoat is dark grey, with gilt cream in old silver applied on top for a denser metallic finish.

COPPER

The warm, reddish tones of copper are extremely decorative and seem to complement decorating schemes of every period. Over time, however, real copper is susceptible to the atmosphere and can take on a dullish brown look before acquiring the greenish patina known as verdigris. Painting objects with a copper effect ensures that they remain permanently bright and glowing in appearance.

1 Mask off any areas that you do not want to get paint on. Rub down the surface with sandpaper to provide a key so that the paint will adhere.

2 Stipple copper enamel paint over the whole surface using the tips of the bristles of a household paintbrush. Leave it to dry.

3 Brush copper gilt cream over the surface of the object.

4 Dab on more copper gilt cream in patches for a fairly solid effect.

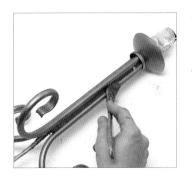

5 Use a dry cloth to buff the surface to a strong shine.

ABOVE: This shallow dish is painted with a gold enamel paint, then stippled with copper enamel and finished with gilt cream.

PEWTER

While new pewter is a shiny silver colour, old pewter takes on a deep grey patina and attractive mellow sheen when buffed. It was once much used in well-to-do households for domestic items such as tankards, flagons and plates. This technique is ideal for transforming ordinary everyday items into decorative accessories that bring a period feel to your kitchen shelves and dining area.

You will need

- sandpaper
- masking tape
- enamel paint in black, white and silver
- household paintbrush

1 Rub down the object with sandpaper to key the surface.

2 Mask off any areas with tape that you do not want to get paint on.

3 Apply a base coat of black enamel paint and leave to dry thoroughly.

4 Lighten the black enamel paint with a little white enamel until you have a dark grey mixture. Using the tips of the bristles of a household paintbrush, stipple this over the whole surface, but in random patches, so that the base coat shows underneath.

5 Mix the dark grey mixture with a little silver enamel paint to lighten it and slightly stipple over the surface in a very patchy manner.

6 Taking silver enamel on its own, stipple the whole surface very lightly with an almost dry brush, just to give a gentle mottled sheen to the surface.

LEFT: *Turn an ordinary vase into a deep pewter one. Apply an undercoat of black enamel paint, then stipple on enamel paint in dark grey and old silver.*

STEEL

Steel is one of the brightest and shiniest of metals and a glint of steel adds a clean and clinical look to a room or object. The technique shown here will enable you to reproduce this modern-looking surface just by applying two types of silver finish and polishing well. Steel is an extremely hard metal, so it is important to achieve a solid paint effect before brushing on gilt cream.

1 Mask off any areas that you do not want to get paint on.

2 Rub down the surface with sandpaper to provide a key so that the paint will adhere.

3 Apply a base coat of bright silver enamel paint. Leave to dry.

4 Apply a second coat of bright enamel silver until you achieve a completely solid effect.

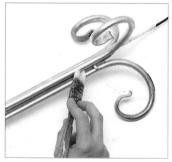

5 When the paint is dry use a soft brush to gently apply bright silver gilt cream over the surface.

6 Buff and shine with a cloth to achieve a highly polished look. Varnish with a high gloss finish.

BELOW: A wooden bowl is transformed with a steel finish. Two coats of bright aluminium enamel paint are applied over a dark grey undercoat. The surface is finished with a gloss varnish.

AGED BRONZE

Few people have authentic ancient or antique bronze items in their house. This paint effect can be used on all manner of ordinary household containers and other items to give the appearance of bronze. With this effect, you can transform simple bowls and plates into attractive pieces that look as if they are precious archaeological finds, yet can be used without undue care around the house.

1 Rub down the object with sandpaper to key the surface so that the paint will adhere.

2 Mask off any areas that you do not want to get paint on.

3 Apply a base coat of black enamel paint to the object.

4 While wet stipple over the surface with the tips of the bristles of a household paintbrush to create an even, mottled effect. Leave to dry thoroughly.

5 Stipple over the whole surface in bronze enamel paint, being careful not to cover the base coat totally.

6 Rub over the surface with bronze gilt cream and then take a dry cloth and buff to a shiny finish.

RIGHT: Candle sconces take on a different look with an aged bronze effect, giving a room a historic feel to it. These have a red oxide primer base coat, with bronze enamel and gilt cream applied on top.

LEATHER

Surfaces covered with leather have an air of distinction and sophistication. Yet you can achieve this look of luxury quite inexpensively with an ingenious combination of satinwood paint, filler and artists' oil colours. In addition, you need have no moral reservations about the source of the material. Real leather can be dyed in any number of colours, so experiment with your own favourite hues.

1 Apply a base coat of pale pink satinwood paint. Leave to dry.

2 Mix pale pink satinwood paint with powdered interior filler (casting plaster) until you have a paste-like mixture. Dab this mixture over the whole surface until it is about 1cm/$\frac{1}{2}$in thick.

3 Stipple over the whole surface with the tips of the bristles of the same household brush used in step 2, texturing the surface. Leave this to dry thoroughly.

4 Brush undiluted crimson artists' oil colour over the whole surface in a fairly thick coat.

5 Stipple to even out, using the same brush as in step 4.

6 Using the flat side of a clean dry sponge, skim over the surface very gently. Apply no pressure but just let the sponge sit on the surface, removing some of the oil from the top layer and highlighting the whole texture. Varnish when dry.

BELOW: Great for studious vegetarians, this leather-look table top is perfect for the study and has a traditional feel to it.

BAMBOOING

If you are eager to reproduce an Asian look in your home, then this technique is ideal. A bamboo effect can be adapted to suit many different forms of decoration, from large expanses of wall to smaller pieces of furniture such as dining chairs and coffee tables. You can paint ordinary pieces of garden cane to make them look more authentic and then use them to make items such as picture frames.

1 Apply two coats of pale yellow satin or gloss finish paint and leave to dry thoroughly.

2 Mix yellow ochre artists' oil colour paint with white spirit (turpentine) into a creamy consistency in a paint kettle (pot). Drag the mixture over the surface. Leave this to dry thoroughly.

3 Measure and draw pencil lines to mark the bamboo panels and then make marks within these about 1.25cm/$\frac{1}{2}$in apart in the direction of the dragging.

4 Once the pencil lines are complete, draw in the slightly rounded ends of the bamboo. Make sure there are not too many of these, or it will look far too complicated when finished.

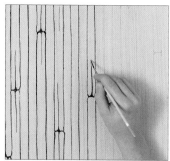

5 Mix burnt umber artists' oil colour paint with white spirit (turpentine) in a small paint kettle (pot) to make a thick cream. Using a lining brush, draw over the pencil lines, adding elongated lines from the middle of the bamboo ends about 10cm/4in long.

6 Flick tiny dots of the burnt umber and white spirit (turpentine) mixture over the surface and soften these with the edge of a brush in the direction of the dragging and the bamboo lines.

BELOW: The furniture and accessories in this room have an Oriental feel to them which is a perfect setting for the bamboo effect on the wall.

MARBLING

There are many specialist (specialty) techniques for achieving a marble effect, but here is a very simple method. Types of marble vary greatly in colour and pattern, and it may be a good idea to use a piece of real marble as a reference source. Aim for a general effect of marbled patterning that is subtle in colour, with most of the veining softened to create depth.

Always use an oil-based gloss or satin base coat to enable the paint to slide and not absorb the colour.

Try colour variations of crimson and ultramarine; raw sienna and black; Indian red, yellow ochre and black; raw sienna, yellow ochre and Prussian blue; Prussian blue and ultramarine; or Naples yellow and yellow ochre.

1 Paint a base coat of white satinwood paint on to the surface. Then squeeze a long blob of ultramarine artists' oil colour paint into a paint kettle (pot) and add some white spirit (turpentine) to form a thick cream. Brush on patches of this.

2 Then squeeze some yellow ochre artists' oil colour paint in to a paint kettle (pot) and dilute it with white spirit (turpentine) until you have a thick cream. Fill in the patches where the blue has not been painted with this mixture.

3 While these colours are wet, take a stippling brush and blend them gently together.

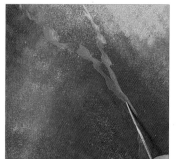

4 Dip a swordliner (liner) brush into white spirit (turpentine) and drag it through the wet surface, applying no pressure but just letting the brushstroke sit on the surface. Slightly angle the bristles while you pull the brush down.

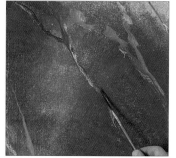

5 Dip the brush back into the white spirit (turpentine) for each line. The white spirit (turpentine) will finally separate the oil glaze surface. Make sure there are not too many lines and only add the odd fork – the less complicated the pattern, the better the effect will be.

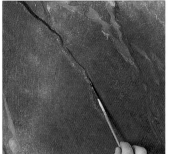

6 Dip the swordliner (liner) into the dark blue glaze remaining from step 1 and draw down the side of each line with a very fine line. Varnish with gloss when dry.

RIGHT: This wooden frame has been changed beyond recognition by using the decorating technique of marbling to give it a patterned border.

MARBLING

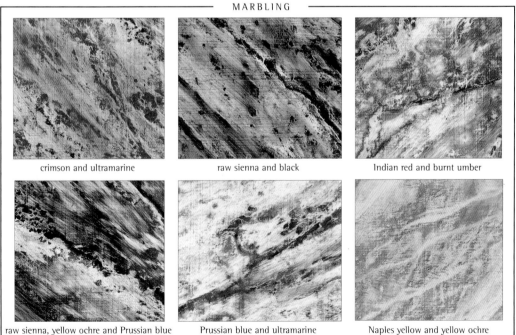

crimson and ultramarine

raw sienna and black

Indian red and burnt umber

raw sienna, yellow ochre and Prussian blue

Prussian blue and ultramarine

Naples yellow and yellow ochre

FLOATING MARBLE

Floating marble is also known as fossil marble, and this is one of the simplest marble effects to reproduce. The technique can only be done on a totally flat surface as the paint and white spirit (turpentine) should not be allowed to run. It relies on many drops of white spirit (turpentine) being spattered over wet oil paint, which then disperses to create tiny veining effects and distortions. The result is a complicated but realistic-looking fossil marble effect with little effort.

Interesting colour variations for this effect are ultramarine and yellow ochre; Indian red, raw sienna and black; crimson, yellow ochre and blue; violet, ultramarine and yellow ochre; burnt umber, raw sienna and Indian red; raw sienna, Prussian blue and violet.

1 Mix Davy's grey artists' oil colour paint with some white spirit (turpentine) in a paint kettle (pot) until you have a thick creamy mixture. Brush this on your surface in random patches.

2 Then mix yellow ochre artists' oil colour paint with some white spirit (turpentine) until it is a thick creamy mixture. Use this to fill in the patches where the grey has not been painted.

3 Add smaller patches of Prussian blue artists' oil colour paint mixed into a thick cream with white spirit (turpentine).

4 While these paints are still wet stipple them together to fuse the colours and blend slightly.

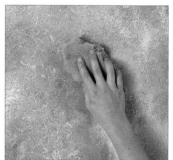

5 Dip a sponge into white spirit (turpentine) and then dab over the surface. The white spirit (turpentine) will begin to disperse the artists' oil colour paint.

6 Dip a brush into white spirit (turpentine) and flick the bristles, spattering the surface. The white spirit (turpentine) will pool and create the fossil stone formation. Varnish with gloss when dry.

RIGHT: This floor is painted with a floating marble technique. The base coat is white satinwood paint, and the colours are achieved with Prussian blue, emerald green and yellow ochre artists' oil colour paint. The effect is protected with varnish.

FLOATING MARBLE

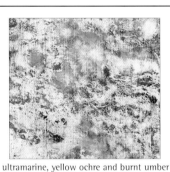

ultramarine, yellow ochre and burnt umber

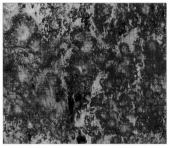

Indian red, raw sienna and black

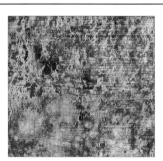

crimson, yellow ochre and blue

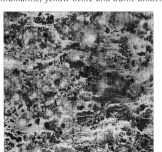

violet, ultramarine and yellow ochre

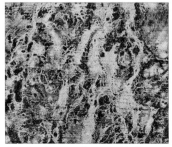

burnt umber, raw sienna and Indian red

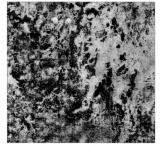

raw sienna, Prussian blue and violet

VERDIGRIS

Verdigris is the beautiful green crust or patina that develops on copper, bronze or brass when it is exposed to the elements. Thus, this effect is suitable for objects both inside and outside the house. It is ideal for disguising and enhancing planters, pots and statuary to add a finishing touch to a conservatory. If the surface is polished with gilt cream it gives a hint of the original bright metal that hides beneath.

1 Rub down the surface with sandpaper to provide a key so that the paint will adhere to it.

2 Apply a base coat of jade green satin or gloss finish paint and leave to dry thoroughly.

3 Lightly stipple bronze enamel paint over the surface using the tips of the bristles of the brush. Make sure that you keep a little of the base coat exposed.

4 Stipple gold enamel paint over the whole surface even more lightly than the bronze layer and in random patches.

5 With a dry brush dab over the surface of the jade green base coat, blending slightly. Leave to dry.

6 Brush a little copper gilt cream over the whole surface with the tips of the brush. Then buff to a strong shine with a dry cloth.

BELOW: The clever use of paint to create a verdigris effect transforms this mirror, as well as helping to hide any imperfections on the original frame.

FAUX PLASTER

The soft texture of new plaster has a warm welcoming feel that is usually lost when covered in many layers of paint. However, this technique shows you how to re-create the look of bare plaster, whether new or old. Two finishes are shown – freshly applied in a textured manner or a distressed, layered surface that looks as if it has seen centuries of wear. Emulsion (latex) paint is used for both effects.

TEXTURED PLASTER

The textured finish of this effect is easily achieved by adding powdered interior filler (casting plaster) to the paint mixture.

You will need

- 10cm/4in household paintbrush
- emulsion (latex) paint in white, dark beige and old white
- interior filler powder (casting plaster)
- wide paintbrush
- paint kettle (pot)

1 Apply a base coat of white emulsion (latex) paint to the surface. Then, using a large brush in random strokes, add dark beige emulsion (latex) to the surface in a roughly painted dry-brush motion, leaving the white base coat showing through beneath.

2 Mix some old white emulsion (latex) in a paint kettle (pot) with powdered interior filler (casting plaster) to make a thick paste. Using a wide brush, apply this to the surface in a roughly painted dry-brush motion as in step 1, alternating the angle of the brush and holding it almost flat to the surface.

3 Continue to apply the paint mixture, making sure that the beige layer of paint is still visible.

4 Using the flat side of the brush, add thicker areas of mixture for a more textured effect.

LEFT: A crisp white finish is added to the textured faux plaster effect to give it the look of a whitewashed cottage.

5 Once dry, dry-brush white paint over the entire surface, picking up the top layer.

6 Without adding any more paint to the surface, gently soften the paint you have added in step 5 with the edge of the brush to complete the textured plaster effect.

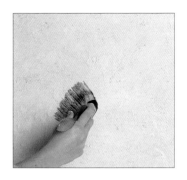

FLAT PLASTER EFFECT

This flat plaster effect, reminiscent of ancient Mediterranean walls, is produced by using methylated spirits (methyl alcohol), which eats into the layers of paint without building up texture on the walls.

You will need
◆ 10cm/4in household paintbrush
◆ emulsion (latex) paint in dark beige, old white and off-white
◆ methylated spirits (methyl alcohol)
◆ cloth/sponge

1 Using a large brush, apply dark beige to the surface with random strokes. Do this by dipping the bristles of a 7.5cm/3in household paintbrush into the paint, scraping off the excess and then loosely applying it to the wall.

2 Using old white emulsion (latex) paint and a large brush, dry brush over the dark beige, leaving some of the base coat exposed. Continue to keep the angle of the strokes random so that the effect looks quite rough.

3 Using off-white emulsion (latex) paint, dry brush over the previous layer in patches.

4 Soften this down with the edge of the brush, hardly adding any paint to the surface. Leave to dry.

5 Soak a sponge in methylated spirits (methyl alcohol) and work it in random patches to wear down the layers of the paint, giving a softer effect.

ANIMAL PRINTS

Animal prints are amazingly versatile as a decoration and are popular with all ages. Of course, they are particularly colourful for children's rooms, but they can be a fun addition to even the most sophisticated of adult decorating schemes. Large expanses of these animal prints can add a touch of the exotic, and there are many other animal patterns that you can try after practising with these techniques for giraffe, zebra and cowhide, such as the leopard print skirting illustrated opposite.

GIRAFFE

It is a good idea to look at some real animals first to check that you are reproducing their patterns correctly. The markings on a giraffe are fairly regular.

You will need

- emulsion (latex) paint in white, yellow, pale yellow and dark brown
- large household paintbrush
- pencil

1 Apply a base coat of white emulsion (latex) paint and allow to dry. Dry brush yellow emulsion (latex) over the surface, leaving some of the white base showing.

2 Once this is dry, repeat with pale yellow emulsion (latex) paint to mottle and soften the effect.

3 Draw random giraffe shapes, leaving about 2.5cm/1in gap between them. Fill in the shapes with dark brown emulsion (latex) paint and leave to dry.

4 Apply a second coat of dark brown emulsion (latex) paint to the shapes so that the colour is solid.

5 Dip a large brush into the pale yellow emulsion (latex) paint and wipe off the excess until the minimum amount of paint is left on the bristles. Holding the brush almost parallel to the surface and applying hardly any pressure, gently wisp over the shapes to knock the slight edge off the dark brown emulsion (latex).

ZEBRA

The distinctive stripes of the zebra needed to be carefully observed to note the way in which they sometimes join together. Black is used over brown to prevent the stripes from looking harsh and add texture to the zebra's coat.

1 Dry brush cream emulsion (latex) paint over the whole surface, leaving a patchy finish. Use a large brush for this.

2 Draw the stripes from a rough central line in an outwards direction, making sure you keep these lines quite wobbly and arched.

3 Dry brush off-white emulsion (latex) paint in between the stripes and working in the direction of the stripes. Leave some of the base coat exposed to give the look of a textured coat.

4 Paint in the stripes with dark brown emulsion (latex). Once dry, roughly paint over the brown stripes with black.

5 Soften the top edge of the stripes with off-white emulsion (latex), flicking the brush inwards from outside.

RIGHT: Create a leopard print on a skirting board by using a foam stamp to print the black shapes over a yellow gloss paint.

COWHIDE

The markings on cowhide can be placed quite randomly and the more varied the shapes you paint, the more realistic will be the overall effect.

You will need

- emulsion (latex) paint in pale beige, pale cream, black and dark brown
- household paintbrush
- pencil

1 Dry brush vertical strokes of pale beige emulsion (latex) paint over the surface.

2 Allow the first layer of paint to dry, then dry brush vertical strokes of pale cream emulsion (latex) paint over the surface. Leave to dry.

BELOW: This frame is decorated with a traditional folk art animal print. The paw prints are made using a dry stencil brush dipped in paint and the effect is finished with a tinted varnish.

3 Draw the shapes of the cowhide in pencil, keeping them random and making sure that plenty of the background remains.

4 Fill in these shapes with black emulsion (latex) paint. Leave to dry.

5 Dry brush a little dark brown emulsion (latex) paint over the black to soften the look slightly, following in the direction of the dry brushing in step 1.

6 When dry, flick along one side from the outside inwards into the shapes with pale cream emulsion (latex) paint to achieve an overlapped fur effect.

TROMPE L'OEIL DOORWAY

Here is a design for a trompe l'oeil doorway that you can follow exactly or use as a guide for your own design. Colours are suggested for you to use, but you may prefer to choose others. The basic techniques used for this doorway could also be used to paint a window or smaller cupboard door. Final details are drawn in with a coloured pencil. By starting with a simple design like this you will soon find that your confidence builds up and you will be able to tackle more complicated designs.

You will need

- paint roller
- emulsion (latex) paint in cream, warm yellow, terracotta and green
- large household paintbrush
- pencil
- set (T) square
- paper
- spirit level (level)
- straightedge
- string
- masking tape
- medium household paintbrush
- medium artist's brush
- hand sander
- brown pencil

1 Experiment with mixing the colours. You can use quite strong shades as they will soften once they have been sanded back.

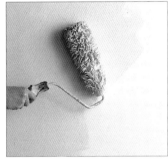

2 Using a paint roller, paint the wall surface with a base coat of cream emulsion (latex) paint.

3 Wash over the base colour with warm yellow emulsion (latex) paint, using a large paintbrush.

LEFT: This effect is simpler to achieve than it looks; its basic shape can be pencilled in with the help of a piece of string used as a pair of compasses and a ruler.

4 Draw your design to scale on paper, using a set (T) square.

5 Draw the straight lines that will represent the doorway and border design on the wall, using a spirit level (level) and straightedge.

6 Draw the upper curve of the doorway, using a pencil tied to a piece of string.

7 Mask off the areas of the design that will be painted in terracotta with masking tape.

8 Paint these areas with the terracotta emulsion (latex) paint, then remove the masking tape. Any smudging can be wiped off immediately.

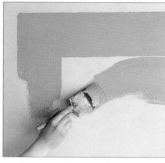

9 Using a medium paintbrush, paint the green areas of the doorway. Use masking tape, if necessary, to mask off each area.

10 Using an artist's brush, paint a thin yellow outline around all the edges of the doorway. Leave to dry.

11 Lightly sand over the design, using a hand sander. Sand down to the base coat in some areas and leave other sections untouched.

12 Wash over the whole design again using warm yellow emulsion (latex) paint.

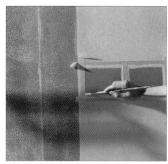

13 Mask off squares in the border area with masking tape. Using an artist's brush, outline each square in yellow, and then immediately remove the masking tape.

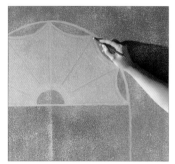

14 Using a brown pencil, draw fine lines in the semicircular fanlight.

RIGHT: *The look of frescoes, faded over the centuries by the hot Italian sun, can be recreated in your own home. The secret is to build up colours in layers and rub them back to different levels.*

TROMPE L'OEIL PANELLING

Using simple trompe l'oeil techniques you can transform your room into any style or period you wish. This simple effect shows you how to paint panels with planked sides and mitred corners. Using lighter and darker tones for the narrow inner panel creates the illusion of light and shadow and gives depth to the frame. You can vary the size of the panels to suit the design of your room.

1 Apply two coats of white emulsion (latex) to make a base coat. Leave to dry between coats. When dry, use a ruler, spirit level (level) and pencil to draw up a central panel with planked sides.

2 Mask off the central panel, running the masking tape all the way up the sides and then across the top and along the bottom of the central panel.

3 Mix 50 per cent beige emulsion (latex) paint with 50 per cent wallpaper paste in a paint kettle (pot). Paint over the central panel and then drag downwards with the brush.

4 Remove the tape from the top and bottom then paint and drag the top and bottom sections horizontally with the same mixture from step 3. Then remove the side tape and drag the panels in a downwards motion.

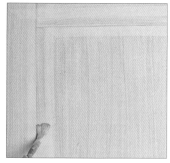

5 Once dried, reapply the tape so that a band of about 2.5cm/1in is created around the central panel, masking the surrounding area off. Mix white emulsion (latex) paint with some of the mixture from step 3 and apply to the sides closest to the light source, mitring the corners with masking tape.

6 Once this is dry, apply tape to mitre the corners in the opposite direction. Mix brown emulsion (latex) paint with some of the mixture from step 3 and apply it to the top and right sides to give the shadows. Remove the tape.

RIGHT: This technique is particularly good for large, bare expanses of wall. The deep red colour used here gives an air of formality which is enhanced by the addition of faux panelling.

TROMPE L'OEIL SKY

This lovely effect is suitable for any room in which you wish to create a sense of calm and imagine yourself floating away among the clouds. Draw the outline shapes of the clouds, but do not feel you have to follow them rigidly. Allow yourself the freedom to paint loose shapes with merging edges for a realistic look. Adding wallpaper paste to the paint gives texture and depth to the whole effect.

You will need

- emulsion (latex) paint in white and sky blue
- sponge
- pencil
- silk finish emulsion (latex) paint in white
- wallpaper paste
- paint kettle (pot)
- household paintbrush

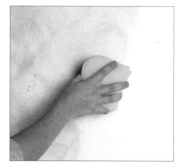

1 Apply two coats of white emulsion (latex) as a base coat, allowing to dry between coats. Dip a sponge into sky blue emulsion (latex) paint and rub over the whole surface in a circular motion, leaving a mottled effect.

2 Apply a second coat of sky blue with a sponge in the same way as step 1. The second coat will leave the whole effect almost solid but with a slightly mottled look.

3 Using a light pencil, carefully outline rough cloud shapes to give a guide to painting.

4 Dilute white silk emulsion (latex) paint with 50 per cent wallpaper paste in a paint kettle (pot) and stipple this onto the surface, starting along the top edge of the pencil line. Continue to stipple downwards without applying any more paint to the brush and this will gradate the colour.

5 Build up the depth of the clouds in layers when each has dried. Go over the first layer along the top side and then stipple downwards as before. This will strengthen the effect.

6 Finally, add a sharper edge to define the white.

BELOW: Add to the sense of light by hanging a mirrored candle holder on the wall that acts as a window into the sky beyond it.

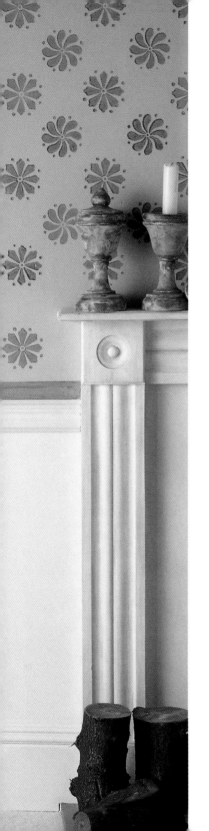

DECORATING
SCHEMES

The most exciting part about using paint effects is planning how they will work together. You may want to decorate a room with a particular theme, or combine specific effects with distinctive colours. The following pages suggest all the factors to consider, and give some ideas for decorating schemes based on colour, patterns and styles from around the world. You can follow the steps for the projects exactly or use elements from them, adapting them to your own taste. Most describe a basic treatment for the walls and show some simple finishes for added decoration.

ABOVE: A flag motif stamped on to the wall of this kitchen instantly gives the room a nautical feel.

OPPOSITE: The pattern on the walls perfectly complements the Scandinavian theme of this living room.

CHOOSING A SCHEME

Before dashing straight for the colour cards and paint pots take time to think exactly what you want to achieve when you decorate your home. You need to consider if the scheme you are choosing will succeed in the room you wish to paint.

Take a good look at the room. Take into account the size and how much light it receives. This can make the difference between a room that receives almost no direct sunlight and one that will be sunny and bright for much of the day. If east or west facing it may receive sunlight only in the morning or afternoon. Light can radically change the appearance of colours. The shape of the room can also have some bearing, as light may be angled more strongly in some areas depending on the position of the windows, doors and alcoves. Make sure you see the colours in the actual room at different times of the day.

Look at the colours that are already in the room. There may be much that you cannot change, such as furniture, carpets and curtains, and you will have to plan your colours and effects around these. Figure out your scheme with these fixed items in mind.

Choose colours and effects for the atmosphere that you want to create – warm and cosy or cool and spacious. They can also be used to give the visual impression of changing the shape of a room. Warm colours seem to advance, so use these if you want to make a room look smaller. Cool colours recede and are

OPPOSITE: The light colours used in this scheme give the kitchen a suitably fresh and airy feel.

BELOW: A wall decoration could be influenced by the soft colours, textures and shapes of a collection of ceramics.

BELOW LEFT: A frottage effect above dado height teams perfectly with wallpaper below. The soft green colour is a restful shade to choose for any room, including a narrow hallway.

ABOVE: Trompe d'oeil *china plates painted over antiqued shelves immediately suggest a country home interior.*

BELOW: A hand-painted and stamped frieze adds colour and decoration to a child's room. Here the frieze is just part of the overall design with the green skirting (base) board standing in for grass and the walls decorated with a sky effect.

useful for making a room look bigger. Similarly, dark tones tend to advance and light tones recede, so use shades of colour to visually move space. For instance, if you have a high ceiling that you wish to appear lower, paint the walls in a dark colour to picture rail height, then white above this and over the ceiling to reduce the wall height. You can also emphasize certain elements in the room in this way.

Patterns can be used to change space, too. Large, bold-coloured motifs tend to attract the eye, so use them in areas that you wish to bring forward. Small muted patterns tend to merge into an overall textured effect unless you are close to them. Vertical patterns such as stripes will give the impression of heightening an area, while horizontal ones will widen it. Remember that texture will also have some effect by breaking up the surface and disguising imperfections.

Bear in mind the age of the building you are decorating. Consider whether a particular style or theme is appropriate to the architecture. There may be existing original features that you can plan a theme around. Perhaps you can adapt elements in the design of the furniture or fittings to create a completely original theme. A motif from the design of the curtains, for instance, can be used as a basis for a stencil or stamp pattern. The overall style of the room could be

ABOVE: *A stamped rose motif on a neutral background is quick and simple to do. The motif has been used again to decorate a cream-upholstered director's chair to pull the scheme together.*

enhanced with faux effects such as verdigris candlesticks, pewter vases or copper plates. Let your imagination run wild.

Flick through magazines and books, find a colour scheme that appeals and see how you can interpret it into your own interior. Try out your ideas on paper – even a rough sketch with the colours and the main elements of the room in place will help you see whether the scheme will work. Use paint samples so that you are accurate in your choice of colour. The more care you take in planning, the more successful the result is likely to be.

The amount of time and money you have available for decorating are important considerations. If you have only limited time, choose an effect that you will be able to complete without leaving the job half done. Practise the paint techniques before starting on a large-scale project for a room. Check that the type of paint you are going to use is suitable for the particular technique you have chosen. Also figure out how much paint and other materials you will need so that the cost for completing the whole scheme falls within your budget.

Another important point to remember is paint safety. Make sure you have all the equipment you need before you start. Take great care when using stepladders. Make sure they are safe before climbing them. Do not lean out in an effort to paint an odd corner, but get down and move the ladder nearer to the place you want to paint. Keep paints and solvents well out of the way of children and animals. Store solvents and thinners tightly capped in their original containers with the relevant labels intact. Put them in a dark, cool area away from heat.

Finally, have fun with your decorating scheme. With careful planning and a bit of practice you will find that not only do you have a new skill, but you can change the interior of your house with the stroke of a brush.

SCANDINAVIAN LIVING ROOM

Create a cool atmosphere with this sophisticated Gustavian-influenced wall stamping. This project requires some preparatory work, but the elegance of the result justifies the little extra time. The stamps are cut from high-density foam or foam rubber which can be mounted on blocks of composition (mat) board with a small drawer knob added for easy handling, if required. Before you do any stamping, draw a grid down the wall using a plumb line and a cardboard square. If you find the effect of the two blues too cool, you can add warmth by applying a coat of tinted varnish to the wall, ageing the whole effect.

You will need

- wood glue
- 2 pieces of composition (mat) board, 9cm x 9cm/3¹/₂in x 3¹/₂in
- 2 pieces of high-density foam rubber, such as upholstery foam, 9cm x 9cm/3¹/₂in x 3¹/₂in
- tracing paper
- pencil
- spray adhesive
- craft knife
- ruler
- 2 small wooden drawer knobs
- plumb line
- cardboard 18cm x 18cm/7in x 7in
- plate
- emulsion (latex) paint in dark blue
- square-tipped paintbrush

1 Apply wood glue to the composition (mat) board squares and stick the foam rubber on to them. Leave to dry.

2 Trace and transfer the shapes from the back of the book. Spray with adhesive and place on the foam rubber.

3 Cut around the edges of the designs and remove the paper pattern. Scoop out the background to leave the stamp free of the composition (mat) board.

4 Draw two intersecting lines across the back of the composition (mat) board and glue a wooden drawer knob in the centre to finish the stamp.

5 Attach a plumb line at ceiling height to give a vertical guideline (this can be done with a piece of masking tape) on the wall. Mark a point 8cm/3¼in above the dado (chair) rail and place one corner of the cardboard square on it, lined up along the plumb line. Mark all the corners of the cardboard square on the wall in pencil, then move it up, continuing to mark the corners. Use this system to mark a grid of squares across the whole surface of the upper wall.

6 One of the stamps has a static motif and the other has a swirl. Use the static one first, dipping it into a plate coated with paint and making the first print on a sheet of scrap paper to make sure that the stamp is not overloaded. Then print up the wall, from the 8cm/3¼in mark.

7 Continue printing, working in a diagonal up the wall.

8 Change to the swirl motif, and stamp this pattern in the spaces between the static motifs.

9 Use a pencil and ruler to draw a line 3.5cm/1½in above the level of the dado (chair) rail, all the way along the stamped section of wall.

10 Fill the space between the pencil line and the dado (chair) rail with diluted dark blue emulsion paint, using a square-tipped paintbrush.

RIGHT: The flat blue wall with its stamp motif creates a dynamic background for the elegant mirrors and the delicate wooden furniture.

RENAISSANCE HALLWAY

Turn your hallway into a dramatic entrance with ornate stencils and rich colours inspired by Renaissance designs. The sponged background is a useful device for creating an illusion of texture to the walls and is in keeping with the ornate look of this scheme. Combine the paint effects on the walls with gold accessories, velvets and braids to complete the theatrical setting. This design would also be ideal for creating an intimate dining room for candlelit dinners, with its warm, romantic colours punctuated by luxurious finishing touches seen in the gilded furniture and refined fabric.

You will need

- ruler
- spirit level (level)
- pencil
- masking tape
- emulsion (latex) paints in pale slate-blue, terracotta and pale peach
- sponges
- stencil brushes
- stencil card (card stock)
- craft knife and cutting mat
- stencil paints in dark grey-blue, terracotta, emerald and turquoise

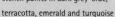

1 Using a ruler and spirit level (level), divide the wall in half horizontally with a pencil line, then draw a second line 15cm/6in above the first. Stick a line of masking tape just below this top line. Dilute one part slate-blue emulsion (latex) with one part water and colour the top half of the wall using a sponge.

2 Stick masking tape just above the bottom pencil line. Dilute terracotta emulsion (latex) paint with water and sponge over the lower half of the wall.

3 Sponge lightly over the terracotta with slate-blue to add a textural effect. Remove the strips of masking tape once you have covered the whole of the wall.

ABOVE: If you are feeling very ambitious, make a matching patchwork cushion cover using pieces of fabric stencilled with gold fabric paint.

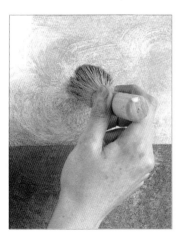

4 Colour the centre band with diluted peach emulsion using a stencil brush. Trace the templates at the back of the book and cut out the stencils from stencil card.

5 Stencil the wall motifs at roughly regular intervals over the upper part of the wall, using dark grey-blue. Rotate the stencil with every alternate motif to give movement to the design.

6 Starting at the right-hand side of the peach band, stencil the border motif with terracotta stencil paint. Add details in emerald and turquoise. Continue along the wall, positioning the stencil beside the previous motif so that the spaces are equal, creating a balanced effect.

RIGHT: *Complete the look with an ornate brass candle holder, fixed to a plain section of wall, between the stencils.*

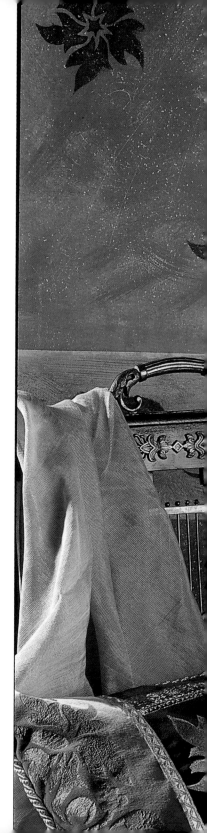

SCANDINAVIAN DOOR PANELS

Painted furniture and fittings are very popular in Scandinavia, especially designs that celebrate nature. These beautiful panels are painted freehand, with flowing brushstrokes. Do not worry too much about making the doors symmetrical – it is more important that the painting should look natural. Practise the strokes with art brushes first on a piece of paper until you feel confident. Any cupboard or dresser doors would be suitable for this design. You could even decorate modern kitchen units.

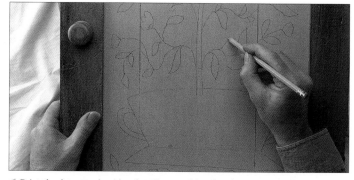

1 Paint the door panels with pale yellow emulsion (latex). Leave to dry. Draw the design on each panel in pencil, using the template at the back of the book.

2 Put some yellow ochre artist's acrylic paint on to a plate. Mix in ultramarine to make grey-green. Using a lining brush, begin painting the design at the top of the first panel.

3 Work your way down the panel, resting your painting hand on your other hand to keep it steady.

4 Put some antique white artist's acrylic paint on to a plate. Using an artist's brush, paint the flowerpot and swirls below. Add the flowers, applying pressure to the brush. Darken the paint with more yellow ochre, then add the soil colouring in the pot.

5 Paint the other panel and leave to dry. Apply a protective coat of clear matt varnish.

RIGHT: *Use this design on a cupboard to create a country theme in a kitchen.*

SCANDINAVIAN BEDROOM

This delicate stamped decoration on walls and woodwork has been applied with a very light touch and is designed to blend in with the pale coloured background and painted furniture so typical of period Scandinavian interiors.

1 Mix the grey-blue emulsion (latex) paint with 50 per cent wallpaper paste and apply to the walls with a broad paintbrush, working at random angles and blending the brushstrokes to avoid hard edges. Allow to dry, then repeat so as to soften the effect.

2 Mix 25 per cent off-white emulsion (latex) paint with 75 per cent wallpaper paste and brush on to the walls as before. Allow to dry.

3 Hang a plumb line 2.5cm/1in from one corner and use as a guide to draw a vertical line down the wall. Measure about 40cm/16in across and draw a second vertical line, again using the plumb line as a guide. Repeat all around the room.

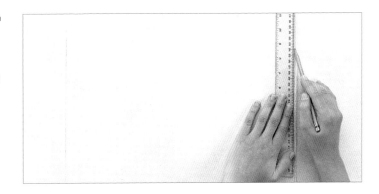

4 Trace the template at the back of the book and transfer it to a rectangle of high-density foam rubber. Cut away the excess sponge around the design using a craft knife.

5 Use a small paint roller to load the stamp with off-white emulsion (latex) paint. Distribute the paint over the whole stamp.

6 Add details in red and grey-blue emulsion (latex) paint, using a paintbrush to add the colours over the off-white paint.

7 Apply the stamp to the wall, positioning it centrally over the marked line. Use the central red tip as a guide. Repeat, positioning the stamp so that each motif is just touching the preceding one. Work down from the top of the wall.

8 Use the grey-blue wash mixed for the wall base coat to drag the door. Do this by applying pressure to the bristles, then pulling down steadily in a straight line, following the direction of the wood grain as you go.

9 Apply the paint to the stamp as before, but this time loading only one flower motif. Stamp a single motif diagonally into the corners of each door panel.

10 Add more paint to the grey-blue wash to deepen the colour and use it to edge the door panels. Leave to dry, then apply two coats of matt varnish to the door to protect the design.

RIGHT: This charming scheme is perfect for the bedroom, creating a restful atmosphere.

MEDIEVAL HALLWAY

A welcoming hallway decorated with medieval patterns and colours will make a stunning entrance to your home. If your hallway seems dark and narrow, using two colours will help make it appear more spacious. A dark colour above dado (chair) rail height creates the illusion of a lower ceiling, while a light colour below, combined with a light floor covering, seems to push the walls outwards to give the impression of width. The crown pattern on the lower half of the wall is stamped in a diagonal grid, which is easy to draw using a plumb line and a square of card (card stock).

You will need

- pencil
- emulsion (latex) paint in dark blue-green, buttermilk yellow and light cream
- paintbrush
- fine-grade sandpaper
- masking tape
- ruler
- paint roller
- wallpaper paste
- plate
- foam roller
- diamond and crown stamps
- plumb line
- card (card stock) measuring 15cm x 15cm/6in x 6in

1 Draw a horizontal pencil line on the wall, at dado (chair) rail height. Paint the top half in blue-green and the bottom in buttermilk yellow emulsion (latex) paint. When dry, lightly sand the blue-green paint. Stick a strip of masking tape along the lower edge of the blue-green, and another 10cm/4in below. Apply light cream paint with a dry roller over the buttermilk yellow.

2 Stick another length of masking
tape 2cm/5in below the one
marking the edge of the blue-green
section. Using a paintbrush and blue-
green paint, fill in the stripe between the
two lower strips of tape. Leave to dry
and peel off the tape. Lightly sand the
blue-green stripe to give it the
appearance of the upper section of wall.

3 On a plate, mix one part blue-green
emulsion (latex) paint with two parts
pre-mixed wallpaper paste and stir well.
Ink the diamond stamp with the foam
roller and stamp a row of diamonds on
the narrow cream stripe.

*BELOW: Basic geometric patterns used at
dado (chair) rail height are a useful
decorative device to separate the different
background colours, above and below.*

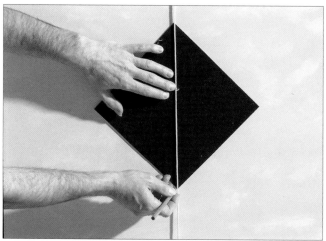

4 Use a plumb line and a card (card stock) square to mark an all-over grid on the cream half of the wall. This will be used as a guide for the crown stamps.

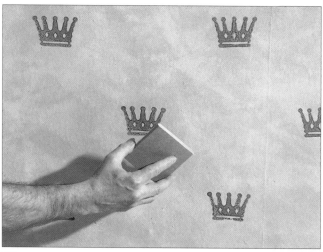

5 Ink the crown stamp with the blue-green emulsion (latex) paint and wallpaper paste mixture and stamp a motif on each pencil mark. Make several prints before re-inking to create variation in the density of the prints.

RIGHT: This themed hallway is perfectly complemented by a medieval-style cupboard with its heraldic stencilled panels.

STAR BATHROOM

T his misty blue colour scheme is ideal for a bathroom or staircase because the lower part of the wall is varnished to provide a practical wipe-clean surface. The tinted varnish deepens the colour and gives it a sheen that contrasts well with the chalky distemper (tempera) above. The stencil is a traditional quilting motif.

You will need

- tracing paper and pencil
- scissors
- spray adhesive
- stencil card (card stock)
- sharp craft knife and cutting mat
- soft blue distemper (tempera) or chalk-based paint
- large decorator's paintbrushes
- straightedge
- spirit level (level)
- clear satin water-based varnish
- Prussian blue artist's acrylic paint

1 Trace the star from the back of the book and cut out. Spray the back with adhesive and stick to the card.

2 Using a craft knife, cut out the star. Cut inwards from the points towards the centre so that the points stay crisp.

3 Taking a corner first, carefully peel away the paper template on the top to reveal the stencil underneath.

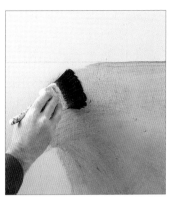

4 Dilute the paint, if necessary, according to the manufacturer's instructions. Brush it on to the wall with sweeping, random strokes to give a colourwashed effect.

5 Using a straightedge and spirit level (level), draw a pencil line across the wall at the height you want to end the darker varnished surface.

6 Tint the varnish with a squeeze of Prussian blue acrylic paint. Using a separate brush, apply this on the lower part of the wall up to the marked line.

7 Spray the back of the stencil with adhesive and position at one end of the wall, 5cm/2in above the marked line. Stencil with the tinted varnish, using a broad sweep of the brush. Repeat along the wall, spacing the stars evenly.

RIGHT: *A classic geometric eight-pointed star is a beautifully simple decoration.*

COUNTRY QUILT FRIEZE

S tamp this friendly, folk-style frieze in a child's bedroom in soft pinks and a warm green. The pattern is reminiscent of an old-fashioned appliqué quilt, and the overlapping edges and jauntily angled birds accentuate its naïve charm. The colour scheme avoids the harshness of primaries, which are so often chosen for children. Green is a calming colour, but it can be cold. For this project use a sap green, which contains a lot of yellow, for warmth. The finished effect is bright enough to be eye-catching without overpowering.

You will need

• emulsion (latex) or artist's acrylic paint in green, sap green, pink and crimson
• paintbrushes
• pencil
• ruler
• spirit level (level)
• tracing paper
• spray adhesive
• medium-density sponge, such as a kitchen sponge
• craft knife
• 4 plates for paint palettes

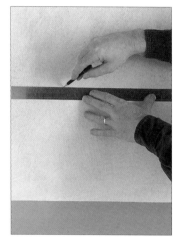

1 Divide the wall by painting the lower section green, up to dado (chair) rail height. Measure 24cm/9½in up from the green section and draw a straight line using a pencil, ruler and spirit level (level) to act as a guide for the top border.

2 Trace the pattern shapes using the templates from the back of the book, then spray the backs with a light coating of adhesive. Stick them on to the foam and cut out with a craft knife. Press the straight strip into green paint and make a test print. Print a line along the pencil guideline, and another just above the green wall section.

3 Press the curved strip into the green
paint, make a test print, then stamp
curved lines to form a branch shape.

4 Press the leaf shape into the green
paint, make a test print, then stamp
the leaves in groups, as shown, two
above and one below the branch.

*BELOW: This charming frieze would work
equally well in a playroom. Since the
design is not too babyish it will last
throughout early childhood.*

5 Stamp pale pink birds along the branch – you need two prints, one facing each direction. Do not make the prints too uniform; aim for a patchy effect.

6 Clean the sponges, then press them into the crimson paint. Stamp the rest of the birds along the branch, alternating the direction of the motif as before.

7 Stamp a row of pink and crimson hearts above the top line to complete the border pattern.

RIGHT: The colours used on the walls are echoed on the door panel, which is painted freehand with a floral design, in keeping with the country theme.

PROVENÇAL KITCHEN

This kitchen is a dazzling example of contrasting colours – the effect is almost electric. Colours opposite each other in the colour wheel give the most vibrant contrast and you could equally well experiment with a combination of blue and orange or red and green. If, however, these colours are just too vivid for you, then choose a gentler colour scheme with the same stamped pattern. The kitchen walls are colourwashed to give a mottled, patchy background. Put some wallpaper paste in the colourwash to make the job a lot easier – it also prevents too many streaks from running down the walls.

You will need

- emulsion (latex) paint in deep purple and pale yellow
- wallpaper paste (made up according to the manufacturer's instructions)
- paintbrush
- plumb line
- cardboard measuring approximately 30cm x 30cm/12in x 12in
- pencil
- plates for palettes
- foam rollers
- rosebud and small rose stamps
- acrylic paint in red and green
- clear matt varnish and brush

1 To make the colourwash, mix one part deep purple emulsion (latex) with one part wallpaper paste and four parts water. Make it up in multiples of six. It is best to make more than you need. Then colourwash the walls. If runs occur, just pick them up with the brush and work them into the surrounding wall, aiming for a patchy, mottled effect.

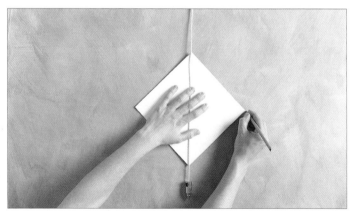

2 Attach the plumb line at ceiling height, just in from the corner. Hold the cardboard square against the wall so that the string cuts through the top and bottom corners. Mark all four points with a pencil. Continue moving the square and marking points to make a grid pattern.

3 Spread some deep purple paint on to the plate and run the roller through it until it is evenly coated. Ink the rosebud stamp and print a rosebud on each pencil mark until you have covered the wall.

4 If you wish to create a dropped-shadow effect, clean the stamp and spread some pale yellow paint on to the plate. Ink the stamp and over-print each rosebud, moving the stamp so that it is slightly off register.

5 Continue over-printing the rosebuds, judging by eye the position of the yellow prints.

▶

BELOW: *Attach a wooden peg rail to the patterned walls to match the Provençal theme.*

6 For the cupboard doors apply a base coat in pale yellow. Spread some green and burnt orange paint on to the plates and run the rollers through them until they are evenly coated. Coat the rose with burnt orange and the leaves with green. (If one colour mixes with the other, just wipe it off and re-coat.) Print a rose in the top left-hand corner. Re-coat the stamp for each print.

7 Print the stamp horizontally and vertically to make a border along the edges of the door panel.

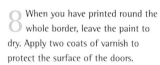

8 When you have printed round the whole border, leave the paint to dry. Apply two coats of varnish to protect the surface of the doors.

RIGHT: *The stamping on the walls and the cupboards instantly transforms a plain kitchen into a busy working one, conjuring up images of delicious French dishes.*

PENNSYLVANIA DUTCH TULIPS

This American folk art inspired idea uses the rich colours and simple motifs inspired by nature and beloved by the German and Dutch immigrants to Pennsylvania. Create the effect of all-over hand-painted wallpaper in a hallway or living room using two different stencil shapes or, for a beginner's project, take a single motif and use it to decorate a key cupboard, a chest of drawers or perhaps the top of a wooden chest.

1 Dilute one part ochre emulsion (latex) with one part water. Using a large paintbrush, cover the top half of the wall with the diluted emulsion (latex). Use vertical brush strokes for an even texture.

2 Paint the lower half of the wall underneath the dado (chair) rail with indigo blue woodwash (wood stain). Finish the surface with a curving line using a dry brush to suggest woodgrain.

3 Paint the dado (chair) rail or a strip at dado-rail height in mulberry woodwash (wood stain) using a narrow brush to give a clean edge.

4 Trace the tulip template from the back of the book and make your own heart template to match. Cut the stencils from stencil card (card stock). Mark the centre of each edge of the stencil. Measure the wall and divide it into equal sections, so that the repeats will fall at about 20cm/8in intervals. Mark the positions lightly with pencil, so that they can be erased later.

5 Dip the stencil brush into red stencil paint. Rub the brush on a saucer or cloth until it is almost dry before stencilling in the tulips. Leave to dry.

6 Paint the leaves in light green stencil paint with darker green shading. Paint the stems in dark green using an artist's brush. Leave to dry.

7 Stencil the tulip basket in pale brown stencil paint using a chunky stencil brush to apply the paint.

8 Stencil a single heart between each two baskets of tulips using red stencil paint and a chunky brush.

9 Decorate a matching key cupboard following the same method and using just one motif in the centre.

RIGHT: These bright country colours will instantly lift a dull hallway, bringing a touch of spring into your home with the use of a charming floral theme.

MEXICAN HALLWAY

B anish gloomy weather with vibrant sunshine yellow and intense sky blue in your hallway. With the heat turned up, add an ethnic touch by stamping an Aztec border along the walls. Use the patterns from the template section to cut basic geometric shapes from a foam rubber sponge, such as the ones used for washing dishes. Mix shades of green with purples, add an earthy red and then stamp on diamonds of fuchsia pink for its sheer brilliance. This makes a bold decorative statement.

Emulsion (latex) paint is available in a wide range of exciting colours. Try not to be tempted by muted colours for this border – it will lose much of its impact. Bright colours go well with natural materials, like straw hats, sisal matting, wicker baskets and clay pots.

You will need

- tape measure
- spirit level (level)
- pencil
- emulsion (latex) paint in sunshine yellow and deep sky blue
- paint roller and tray
- small amounts of emulsion (latex) paint in light blue-grey, purple, brick-red, fuchsia pink and dark green
- 5 plates
- foam rubber sponge

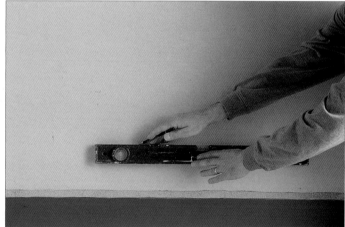

1 Divide the wall at dado (chair) rail height using a tape measure, spirit level (level) and pencil. Paint the upper part in sunshine yellow and the lower part in deep sky blue, using a paint roller. Then use the spirit level (level) and pencil to draw a parallel line about 15cm/6in above the blue section.

2 Use the templates from the back of the book to make the foam rubber stamps for this project. Then stamp a light blue-grey line directly above the blue section. Use this strip again to stamp the top line of the border along the pencil line.

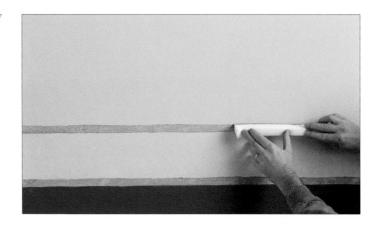

3 Spread an even coating of each of the frieze colours on to separate plates. Use the rectangular and triangular shapes alternately to print a purple row above the bottom line and below the top line. Stamp on to a piece of scrap paper first to make sure that the stamp is not overloaded.

4 Stamp the largest shape in brick red, lining it up to fit between the points of the top and bottom triangles. There should be approximately 1.25cm/½in of background colour showing between this brick-red shape and the triangles.

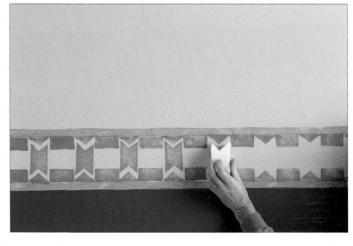

5 Stamp the diamond shapes in fuchsia pink, placing the stamps centrally between the brick-red motifs already stamped.

6 Finally, add a zigzagged edge along the top and bottom by overprinting dark green triangles along the light blue-grey lines.

RIGHT: *The rustic wooden furniture adds an authentic touch to this Mexican setting.*

SANTA FE LIVING ROOM

A ztec motifs, like this bird, are bold, stylized and one-dimensional, and translate perfectly into stamps. Strong colour contrasts suit this style, but here the pattern is confined to widely spaced stripes over a cool white wall, and further restrained with white paint dry brushed over the stamped motifs.

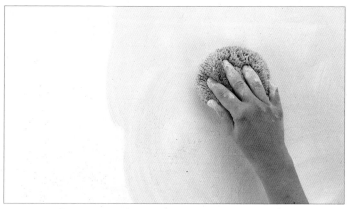

1 Dilute the off-white emulsion (latex) with 50 per cent water and, using a sponge, apply a wash over the wall in an overlapping circular motion. Allow to dry.

2 Using a broad, dry brush, apply warm white emulsion in some areas of the wall to achieve a rough-looking surface. Allow to dry.

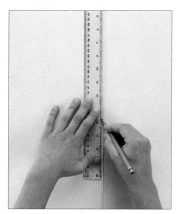

3 Starting 10cm/4in from one corner, and using a plumb line as a guide, draw a straight line from the top to the bottom of the wall.

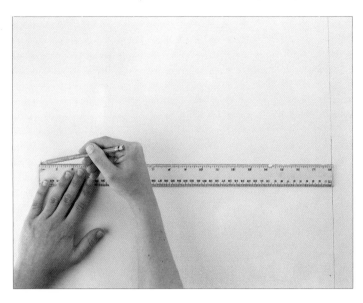

4 Measure 45cm/18in along the wall, hang the plumbline again and mark a second vertical line. Draw another line 10cm/4in away to create a band. Repeat all across the wall.

5 Apply masking tape to the wall on each outer edge of the marked bands.

6 Paint the bands in deep red emulsion (latex) paint. Leave to dry.

7 Draw a 10 x 20cm/4 x 8in diamond shape on a medium-density sponge and cut out the shape using a craft knife and cutting mat.

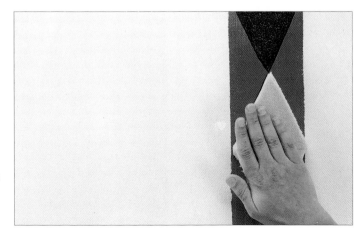

8 Use a small roller to load the stamp with navy blue emulsion (latex) paint and stamp the diamonds down the red bands, starting from the top. Re-coat for each stamp.

9 Copy the bird template at the back of the book on to a piece of high-density foam rubber. Cut away the excess sponge using a craft knife.

10 Use the roller to load the bird stamp with off-white emulsion (latex) and print the birds upright, roughly in the centre of the diamonds.

11 When the motifs are dry, use minimal pressure and a dry brush to brush gently over each band with warm white emulsion (latex) paint.

RIGHT: The paint effects are combined with wooden furniture to complete this look.

INDIAN BEDHEAD

T he inspiration for this arch-shaped bedhead (head board) comes from Indian temple wall paintings. The bedroom feels as if it has been magically transported thousands of miles, but the real magic here comes in a simple pot of paint. Before painting the bedhead (head board), set the mood with a deep rust-coloured wash on the walls. If you can, use a water-based distemper (tempera) for an authentic powdery bloom. If you are using emulsion (latex) paint, thin it with water and use random brushstrokes for a patchy, mottled look. The arch is simply chalked on to the wall using a paper template.

You will need

- large roll of brown parcel wrap (packing paper)
- felt-tipped pen
- masking tape (optional)
- scissors
- spray adhesive
- chalk
- water-based paint in dark blue, bright blue and red
- plate and kitchen sponge
- emulsion (latex) paint in sandy cream
- medium and fine paintbrushes
- fine-grade sandpaper

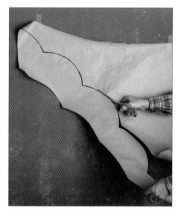

1 Tape a sheet of brown parcel wrap (packing paper) on the wall and draw the half-arch directly on to it, following the pattern shape. Cut out the half-arch shape using a pair of scissors.

2 Position the paper pattern on the wall with spray adhesive and draw around the edges with chalk.

3 Remove the pattern from the wall, flip it over and position it on the opposite side to produce the shape for the second half of the arch. Draw around the edges as before.

4 Spread some dark blue paint on to a plate and use a damp sponge to dab it on to the central panel. Do not cover the background completely but leave some of the wall colour showing through. When the paint is dry, apply the bright blue paint over the dark blue in the same way.

5 When the paint is dry, paint the arch in sandy cream emulsion, using a medium-size paintbrush.

6 When the sandy cream paint is dry, rub it back in places with fine-grade sandpaper, to give a faded effect.

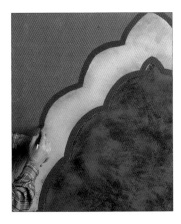

7 Outline the inside and outside of the arch with red paint, using a fine paintbrush. Support your painting hand with your other hand. Use the width of the brush to make a single line.

8 Outline the outer red stripe with a thinner dark blue line. Work as described in the previous step, keeping the line as clean as possible.

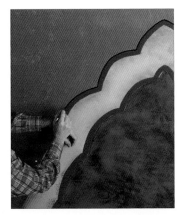

9 Leave to dry, then use fine-grade sandpaper to soften any hard edges so that the arch has the naturally faded appearance of an old temple wall.

RIGHT: A painted head board instantly tranforms the simplest of beds into an item of furniture with a definite style.

POTTING SHED

Create the relaxing atmosphere of a rural potting shed in a hallway where you keep all the clutter needed for use in the garden. Here, broken-colour techniques are used, adding layers of paint to produce a gentle, muted look to the surroundings. The wall is dry brushed in a downward dragging motion to give a softly textured effect. Four layers of colours are used to give depth to the effect as each coat is allowed to show through. The window box and the individual plant pots are given a verdigris finish to make them stylish for decorative use.

1 Apply a base coat of white emulsion (latex) paint to the wall and leave to dry. Dip the tip of a large household paintbrush into cream emulsion (latex) paint, scrape off the excess and apply to the wall in long vertical strokes. Vary the starting point with each stroke and allow the base coat to show through. Leave to dry thoroughly.

2 Then, dip the tip of the paintbrush into moss green emulsion (latex) paint and scrape off the excess. Dry brush the paint on to the wall using long vertical strokes. Make sure that the layer of colour underneath shows through. Leave to dry.

Similarly, dry brush a layer of sage green emulsion (latex) paint using vertical strokes and allowing the underlayers to show through. Leave to dry thoroughly.

4 Finally, when dry, dry brush a layer of cream emulsion (latex) paint in a similar manner to steps 2 and 3.

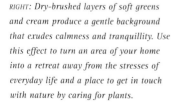

RIGHT: Dry-brushed layers of soft greens and cream produce a gentle background that exudes calmness and tranquillity. Use this effect to turn an area of your home into a retreat away from the stresses of everyday life and a place to get in touch with nature by caring for plants.

5 To prepare the window box for
decorating, rub down the surface
with sandpaper to provide a key so that
the paint will adhere. Apply a base coat
of jade green satin or gloss finish paint
and leave to dry thoroughly.

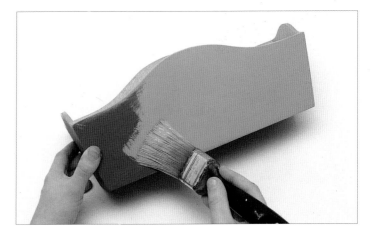

6 Lightly stipple bronze enamel paint
over the surface using the tips of the
bristles of the brush, making sure that
you keep the base coat exposed.

7 Stipple gold enamel paint over the
whole surface even more lightly than
the bronze layer and in random patches.

8 With a dry brush, dab over the
surface of the jade green base coat,
blending slightly. Leave to dry. Rub a
little copper gilt cream over the whole
surface with the tips of the brush. Then,
buff to a strong shine with a dry cloth.

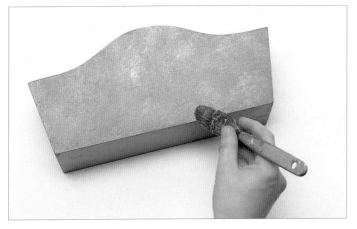

*RIGHT: The colours used in this
arrangement are kept light and are
enhanced by the harmoniously painted
furniture and accessories.*

JAPANESE LIVING ROOM

Roller fidgeting is used to create the warm-looking walls of this traditional Japanese-style living room. Two paint colours mix and merge on the wall as they are applied, providing an ideal ground for a simple freehand leaf design. Painted bamboo panels worked in richer artists' oil colours add an air of authenticity and are fun to paint. Finally the furniture is given a smooth lacquered finish to complement the setting.

1 Apply a coat of off-white emulsion (latex) paint to the wall and leave to dry thoroughly.

2 Pour sand yellow and pale cream emulsion (latex) paint into each side of a roller tray. Coat a masonry roller with the paint and apply it to the wall at random angles, making sure that you do not totally cover the base coat.

3 When the wall is dry mark with a pencil the height and position of the leaf spray border design. Take into account the width of the bamboo panels which will alternate between the leaves. Draw these in at the same time. Draw the centre lines, making sure they are equally spaced around the room, then draw in the leaves freehand.

4 Use an artist's brush to paint in the main stalk in plum emulsion (latex).

5 Paint in the leaves in plum emulsion (latex) paint. Some parts of the leaf spray design may need a second coat.

6 Mask off each of the panels. Apply two coats of pale yellow satin or gloss finish paint and leave to dry thoroughly. Mix yellow ochre artists' oil colour paint with white spirit (turpentine) into a creamy consistency in a small paint kettle (pot). Drag the mixture over the surface. Leave this to dry thoroughly.

7 Measure and draw pencil lines about 1.25cm/½in apart in the direction of the dragging. Once the pencil lines are complete, draw in the slightly rounded ends of the bamboo. Make sure there are not too many of these or it will look far too complicated when finished.

8 Mix burnt umber artists' oil colour paint with white spirit (turpentine) in a paint kettle (pot) to make a thick cream. Using a fine lining brush, draw over the pencil lines adding elongated lines from the middle of the bamboo ends about 12.5cm/5in long. Flick tiny dots of the paint over the surface, and soften with the edge of a brush, moving downwards.

9 To prepare the surface of the table, first sand it thoroughly until totally smooth. Clean the surface, making sure that it is completely free of dust. Apply a base coat of high gloss paint and leave to dry thoroughly. Sand the surface again to ensure total smoothness.

10 Apply a second base coat. Leave to dry thoroughly.

11 Spray on a gloss enamel in the same colour as the base coat. Again, leave to dry thoroughly. Spray a gloss varnish over the surface to protect it and provide a final finish.

RIGHT: The table is lacquered in plum-coloured paint to match the leaf design on the walls. This colour provides a sophisticated contrast to the warm creamy yellow of the walls and darker ochre tones of the bamboo panel without looking too overpowering.

CHURCH HALLWAY

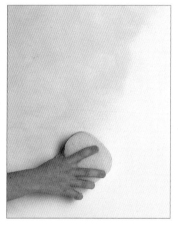

Turn your hallway into a welcoming area of serenity by decorating the walls with a dressed-stone effect reminiscent of an old country church. This easy technique relies on precision in drawing a grid to mark out the individual blocks before painting them in. Consistent edges of highlight and shadow define the blocks. To emphasize the church-like look, the cupboard is painted with a dark oak effect. The rich depth of colour of solid oak is achieved by using burnt umber artists' oil colour paint.

You will need

- sponge
- emulsion (latex) paint in stone yellow, off-white and beige
- spirit level (level)
- pencil
- paint kettle (pot)
- wallpaper paste
- 1.25cm/½in flat end paintbrush
- wooden cupboard
- gloss or satin finish paint in beige
- artists' oil colour paint in burnt umber
- white spirit (turpentine)
- fine graduated comb
- heart grainer (graining roller)
- cloth
- large paintbrush
- varnish

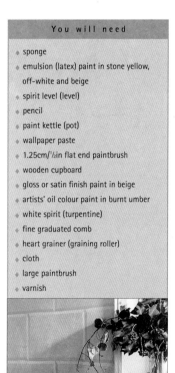

1 Dip a sponge into stone yellow emulsion (latex) and apply to the wall in a circular motion, creating an overall mottled effect.

2 Add a second coat of the stone yellow emulsion (latex) in patches and leave to dry. This will create a slight movement in the overall effect but will look almost solid.

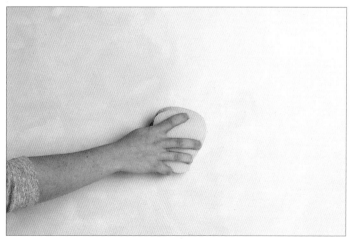

3 Using a spirit level (level), draw a
grid simulating the blocks to achieve
a straight and accurate grid for the stone
blocking effect.

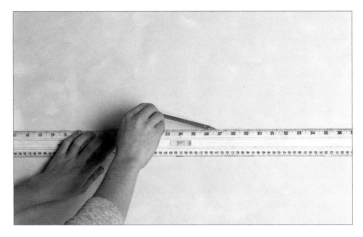

4 Mix off-white emulsion (latex) paint
with 50 per cent wallpaper paste in
a small paint kettle (pot). Using a
1.25cm/½in flat end paintbrush, paint a
stroke across the top and right side of
each block. Leave to dry.

5 Make sure the mitred corners are
painted crisply.

6 Mix beige emulsion paint with 50 per
cent wallpaper paste in a small paint
kettle (pot). Use the same flat end
paintbrush to paint along the bottom
and left of each block. Mitre each corner
which joins the highlight.

7 To paint the cupboard, apply two coats of beige for the base coat in either gloss or satin finish and leave to dry thoroughly. Mix burnt umber artists' oil colour paint with white spirit (turpentine) in a paint kettle (pot) until it is the consistency of thick cream. Brush on and drag in a lengthways direction.

8 Using a graduated comb, pull down on the surface, not in totally straight lines, butting one up against the other.

9 Use a heart grainer (graining roller) to start making the details of the graining. Do this by pulling the tool down gently with a slight rocking motion, to create the hearts with random spacings. Butt one line straight over the other. Using a fine graduated comb, comb over all the previous combing.

10 Wrap a cloth around the comb and dab on to the surface to create the angled grain, pressing into the wet paint. Then, soften the overall effect using a large dry brush. Varnish when dry.

RIGHT: Enhance the church-like effect of the dressed-stone blocking by adding a formal flower arrangement and accessories such as old leather-bound books. Plain church candles are readily available and give a gentle glow at night when lit.

EGYPTIAN BATHROOM

Here, a roller fidgeting technique is ideal for establishing the impression of a slightly textured surface and disguising any small imperfections in the plaster. This bathroom is decorated with Egyptian fan motifs that are carefully measured and drawn before being painted in. The shapes are masked to make painting them in easier and then outlined with paint to make them stand out clearly. Decoration within the motifs is made with a comb while the paint is still wet.

You will need

- emulsion (latex) paint in pale yellow, off-white, orange and turquoise
- wallpaper paste
- paint kettle (pot)
- large paintbrush
- pencil
- long ruler
- drawing pin
- string
- masking tape
- rubber or plastic comb
- lining brush

1 Roller fidget the background using pale yellow and off-white in the same way. When dry, mark out the fan shapes in pencil. Do this with the aid of a long ruler, measuring and marking either side of a centre vertical line. Secure a piece of string to the centre line with a drawing pin and attach the pencil to the other end to draw an arc for the top of the fan. Similarly measure and mark the smaller half fans.

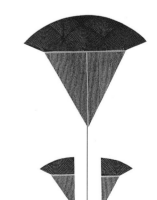

2 Carefully mask off the lower part of each fan (the triangular shape) with masking tape and brush over the enclosed area with a layer of orange emulsion (latex) paint.

3 Immediately, and before the paint has dried, comb over the orange colour in a downwards vertical direction, keeping your hand steady so that the lines are straight. Leave to dry.

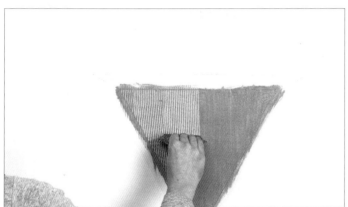

4 Mask off the top part of each fan and brush over with turquoise emulsion (latex) paint, until the enclosed area is completely covered.

5 Again, comb immediately. To achieve the semi-circle patterns, start by angling the comb and your wrist on the left and arc with the top, without moving the bottom of the comb. Leave to dry.

6 Mix some off-white emulsion (latex) paint with a little water until you have a thin creamy mixture. Use this mixture with a lining brush to paint a thin line around all the coloured shapes to clean up any untidy edges. Finally, paint in the centre line of the large fans and the supporting lines of the half fans.

RIGHT: These Egyptian fan motifs are painted in the typical colours of orange and turquoise used by the ancient Pharaohs. These colours were originally made from natural clays and minerals, and their earthy tones are complemented by the pale yellow colourwashed wall. The vibrant look is completed with the addition of colourful shutters and bright accessories.

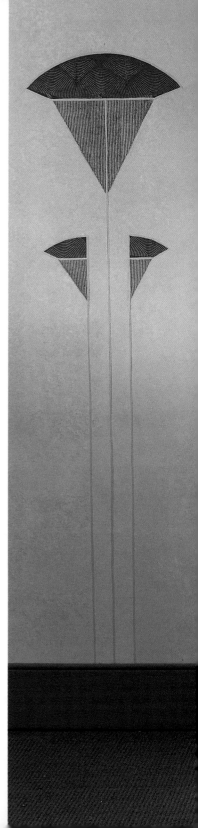

TARTAN (PLAID) STUDY

A warm-looking and well-ordered study is an encouragement to settle down to some writing, reading or serious contemplation! Time-honoured plaids exude a feeling of comforting reliability and a tartan border is much less complicated to paint than you might think. Again, careful measuring is the secret to success and you can use this technique to design any number of combinations of colours and checks. Antique office furniture is expensive, but it is a simple matter to paint an inexpensive desk with a dark wood effect and an attractive leather inset.

You will need

- emulsion (latex) paint in claret red and dark green
- household paintbrush
- long ruler and pencil
- low tack masking tape
- mini paint roller
- acrylic paint in gold
- swordliner (liner) brush
- desk or table
- satinwood paint in pale pink
- interior filler powder (casting plaster)
- artists' oil colour paint in crimson
- synthetic sponge
- varnish

1 Apply two coats of claret red emulsion (latex) paint to the walls that you wish to decorate. Leave to dry.

2 Decide how wide and deep you wish the tartan (plaid) border to be. Then measure and mark it out with a pencil. Taking into account the widths of the roller, mask off the horizontal edges with low-tack masking tape.

3 Measure and mark out a grid for the main check by drawing in the vertical lines, again taking into account the width of roller you will be using.

4 Coat the mini roller with dark green emulsion (latex) paint and pull along the horizontal pencil lines. Leave to dry.

5 Add the vertical lines in dark green using the mini roller.

6 Dilute gold acrylic paint with water until you have a thin creamy mixture. Using this mixture with a lining brush, paint a thin line about 2.5cm/1in to the right of each vertical green line. Leave to dry.

7 Using the same thin mixture of gold acrylic paint and the swordliner (liner) brush, paint a thin line 2.5cm/1in below each horizontal green line.

8 Paint the whole desk in a dark oak effect and leave to dry. Draw a large rectangle on the top and mask off. Apply a base coat of pale pink satinwood paint and leave to dry. Mix pale pink satinwood paint with powdered interior filler (casting plaster) until you have a paste-like mixture. Dab this mixture over the whole surface until it is about 1cm/½in thick.

9 Stipple over the whole surface with the tips of the bristles of the same household brush used in step 8, texturing the surface. Leave this to dry thoroughly.

10 Brush undiluted crimson artists' oil colour paint over the surface in a fairly thick coat. Stipple to even out, using the same brush as in step 9.

11 Using the flat side of a clean dry sponge, skim over the surface very gently. Apply no pressure but just let the sponge sit on the surface, removing some of the oil from the top layer and highlighting the whole texture. Varnish when dry.

RIGHT: *The deep colours chosen for the tartan (plaid) border complement and provide a contrast for the walls of the study, creating a co-ordinated scheme. Borders and bands of checks can define the shape of a room. Placing a horizontal border immediately under the window helps to emphasize the width of the room.*

COLONIAL LIVING ROOM

O ne of the easiest methods for creating a wood panel effect is to use the technique of
dragging. Simply pull the wet paint with the tips of the bristles of a dry brush in the
direction of the wood grain. The technique creates maximum impact in rooms where large
areas of panelling are required, such as this Colonial-style living room. It is important to
keep the lines in each vertical or horizontal section clean and unbroken, so make sure
you plan panels that can be covered with a comfortable stroke of the brush.

You will need

◆ emulsion (latex) paint in off-white and
  mid (medium) brown
◆ household paintbrush
◆ long ruler
◆ pencil
◆ masking tape
◆ wallpaper paste
◆ paint kettle (pot)
◆ soft artist's brush
◆ cloth

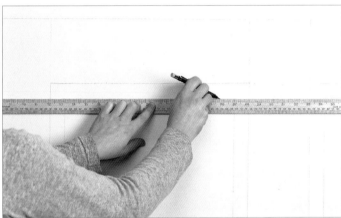

1 Apply two coats of off-white emulsion (latex) paint over the whole wall. Leave to
dry. Measure and mark the height and size of the panelling you require with the
ruler and pencil. Make sure the proportions balance well across the length of the wall.

2 Mask off the dado (chair) rail. Mix
mid brown emulsion (latex) paint
with 50 per cent wallpaper paste in a
paint kettle (pot). Brush the paint
mixture over the dado (chair) rail area.
Using a dry brush, drag along the middle
of the rail in a horizontal direction to
remove some of the paint and create a
highlight effect. Apply masking tape to
the borders of the main panels, mitring
the corners, then paint and drag the
centre panel in a vertical direction.

3 Mask off the top and bottom sections, and paint and then drag them in a horizontal direction.

4 Remove the tape except from the centre panel border. Brush the brown paint mixture on to the side panels and drag down in a vertical direction. Leave the paint to dry.

LEFT: Masking with mitred edges enables you to drag right up to the corners with precision. The highlights and shadows give the illusion of depth. You can achieve the effect easily by mitring the masking tape before applying it, then removing it length by length as you paint each edge.

5 Remove the tape from the bottom of the centre panels and paint in a second coat of the brown mixture to give a darker shadow effect, using a soft artist's brush. Repeat the process for the right-hand side (assuming the light source is from the left).

6 Remove the tape from the left of the centre panels and paint in a coat of the brown mixture, dragging the brush along the inner edge. To create a highlight, take a cloth, while the paint is still damp, wrap it over your index finger and run this along the band removing most of the paint. Repeat the process for the top side (assuming the light source is coming in from the left).

RIGHT: Leather furniture and dark wooden accessories perfectly complement the effect of the wood panels, further enhancing the authenticity of the colonial setting.

SEASIDE KITCHEN

Bring the look of happy seaside vacations into your kitchen throughout the year. The wall is colourwashed using two layers of the same colour to produce an effective backdrop of movement and depth. Simple beach flag motifs are stamped on the wall in a casual manner to reflect the coastal theme, and details painted in with a small brush. The flaking paint on the cupboard is the result of applying a crackle-glaze medium between the two layers of colour on the panels and dry brushing.

You will need

- emulsion (latex) paint in white, mid (medium) blue and yellow
- decorator's brush
- wallpaper paste
- paint kettle (pot)
- mini roller
- flag stamp
- artist's brush
- cupboard
- household paintbrush
- crackle-glaze medium

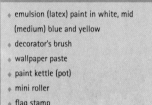

1 Apply a base coat of white emulsion (latex) paint to the wall. Leave to dry. Mix mid (medium) blue emulsion (latex) paint with 50 per cent wallpaper paste in a paint kettle (pot). Apply the mixture to the wall at random angles using a broad decorator's brush and allowing the base coat to show through.

2 When the first layer of blue colourwash is dry, apply a second coat, again in random directions.

3 Using a mini roller, apply a good coat of white emulsion (latex) paint to the raised surface of the stamp.

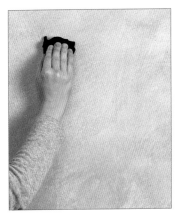

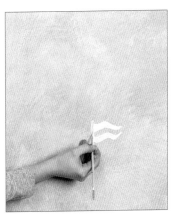

4 Decide where you are going to place the stamp, position it and then press firmly on the wall.

5 Continue to apply stamps to the wall, placing them randomly and making sure that one motif is not directly positioned directly in line with another.

6 When you have completed the stamping use an artist's brush to paint the flagpoles in yellow emulsion (latex) paint to complete the motifs.

7 To decorate the cupboard, apply two base coats of mid (medium) blue emulsion (latex) paint to the outside. Leave to dry.

RIGHT: Cupboards and other small items of furniture are easy to treat with a crackle-glaze effect. Use it to reproduce surfaces that are reminiscent of beach huts exposed to salt and the extremes of the elements through rain and shine.

8 When the blue paint is dry, apply a good coat of crackle-glaze medium to the centre panel, following the manufacturer's instructions.

9 Paint a good coat of white emulsion (latex) over the area where you applied the crackle-glaze medium. Do not overbrush, since the medium will react with the paint fairly quickly to produce the crackle effect. Leave to dry upright to achieve a dramatic cracking effect.

10 Complete the surround to the cupboard panel by scraping the excess white paint from the brush and dry brushing along the edging in the direction of the grain of the wood.

RIGHT: The seaside theme is continued in the accessories in the kitchen, with bright striped china and wooden boats. Plain white shelving can be given an antiqued effect or made from leftover pieces of wood that have been washed up on the shore.

NEO-CLASSICAL BATHROOM

After a hard day's work, transport yourself to the relaxing atmosphere of the ancient Roman baths but with all the conveniences of modern living. This old cast-iron bath (bath tub) is painted with a marble effect on the outside that is easy to achieve, with enamel paint used as a base coat. Use a swordliner (liner) or feather to paint in veins, then soften them off for a realistic subtle look. The wall panels are given a light trompe l'oeil sky effect, so that you have the impression of looking through columns or open window spaces to the exhilarating fresh air outside.

You will need

- cast-iron bath (bath tub)
- suitable enamel paint in white
- household paintbrush
- artists' oil colour paint in Davy's grey (medium gray)
- white spirit (turpentine)
- paint kettle (pot)
- swordliner (liner) or feather
- large softener (blending) brush
- varnish in gloss finish
- emulsion (latex) paint in white and sky blue
- silk finish emulsion (latex) paint in white
- sponge and pencil
- wallpaper paste

1 To decorate the bath tub, apply two coats of white enamel paint to the outer surface of it.

2 Mix a little Davy's grey (medium gray) artists' oil colour paint with white spirit (turpentine) in a small paint kettle (pot) until it has a thin creamy consistency. Use this mixture to paint in the fine veins of the marble with a swordliner (liner) or a feather.

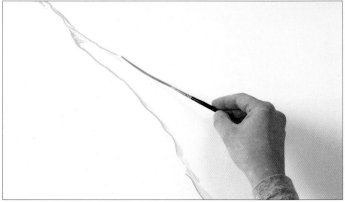

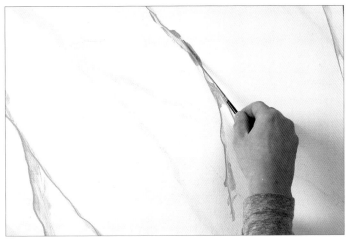

3 Soften the veins using a large soft brush to sweep over the lines.

4 Add more veins, disregarding the positions of the first ones but working in the same general direction.

5 Soften these new veins with the large soft brush using only a little pressure this time, to give these ones a slightly stronger edge.

6 Using the swordliner (liner), add a defining line along the side of the second set of veins. Pull the softening brush along these once if slightly heavy. Leave to dry. Varnish in a gloss finish.

7 To paint the walls, apply two coats of white emulsion (latex) as a base coat, allowing to dry between coats. Measure, draw and mask off the panels. Dip a sponge into sky blue emulsion (latex) paint and rub over the panel in a circular motion, leaving a mottled effect. Once dry, apply a second coat of sky blue with a sponge in the same way. The second coat will leave the whole effect almost solid but slightly mottled in appearance.

8 Using a light pencil, carefully outline rough cloud shapes to give a guide for painting.

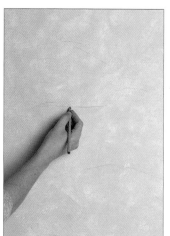

9 Dilute white silk emulsion (latex) paint with 50 per cent wallpaper paste in a paint kettle (pot) and stipple this on to the surface, starting along the top edge of the pencil line. Continue to stipple downwards without applying any more paint to the brush and this will gradate the colour. Build up the depth of the clouds in layers when each has dried: go over the first layer along the top side and again stipple downwards. This will strengthen the effect.

10 Finally add a sharper edge to define the white.

RIGHT: This wonderful trompe l'oeil sky is glimpsed through window shapes and adds the illusion of space to the bathroom. Try it also on ceilings. The luminous quality is achieved by working down the surface several times, gradating the colour as you progress without adding more paint to the brush.

MANHATTAN DINING ROOM

This minimalist, yet striking, striped wall provides an interesting backdrop to a room that is a haven away from the hubbub of city life. The impact of these wide stripes is maximized by taking them right over the skirting (base) board to floor level. A plain beech effect is used to paint the table top, and the surface pattern and texture is achieved by using a heart grainer (graining roller) and comb. The techniques are easy to master. Finally, remember to varnish the table to protect your handiwork.

1 Apply two coats of off-white emulsion (latex) paint to the wall. Leave the paint to dry completely.

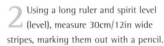

2 Using a long ruler and spirit level (level), measure 30cm/12in wide stripes, marking them out with a pencil.

3 Paint in alternate bands using a wide paint pad and taupe emulsion (latex) paint. Concentrate on the edges before filling the inside of the bands. The paint pad should be well coated, but not over loaded. Press firmly whle pulling down the pencil line to achieve an accurate line.

4 To paint the beech-effect table, apply two coats of white satinwood paint as a base coat. Leave each to dry before applying the next. Mix Naples yellow artists' oil colour paint with white spirit (turpentine) until you have a mixture the consistency of thick cream, then brush it evenly over the surface.

5 Drag the surface in a single, lengthways direction.

6 Use a heart grainer (graining roller) to start making the graining. Do this by pulling the tool down gently, slightly rocking it and working in several spaced lines. Do not butt the lines up together.

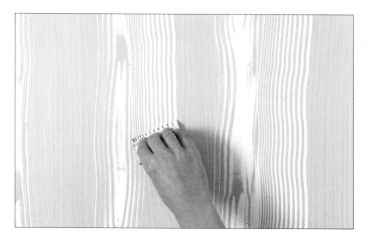

7 With a graduated comb, work in the same direction and fill in the lines between the heart graining.

8 Again, working in the same direction, soften the effect with a large dry brush.

9 Now take a narrow comb and go over the entire surface in the same direction to add detail to the effect. Repeat this until fine lines are achieved. Varnish when dry.

RIGHT: Beech is a light-coloured wood much used for modern furniture and this effect tones well with the stripes on the wall. Although all the colours are neutral in this room, they are varied and warm looking. Choose simple shapes for accessories to enhance the overall contemporary look.

WHERE TO USE SPECIAL EFFECTS

Agate
Use on small objects that would realistically be made from agate.

Ageing/Antiquing
Use to mimic age on painted or bare woodwork.

Animal prints
Each of the zebra, cowhide and giraffe patterns is quite "loud", so use them sparingly, probably with a plain scheme.

Bambooing
Use where bamboo would realistically be used.

Basket weave
Walls are suitable for this effect, which is a controlled version of colourwashing.

Beech
Use where beech would realistically be used.

Bronze
Use on objects that might realistically be made from bronze.

Colourwashing
A basic effect often used for walls. Can also be done on furniture with a different paint mix, using eggshell finish mixed with 50 per cent white spirit (turpentine).

Combing
Can be used on various surfaces. An integral part of woodgraining

Copper
Use on objects that might realistically be made from copper.

Crackle glaze
Furniture is suited to this medium. In most cases it must be used with emulsion (latex) paint, so several coats of varnish are necessary.

Distressing
Use to imitate old painted woodwork, worn and chipped away. Suitable for wood.

Dragging
Traditionally used for woodwork (doors, door and window frames, skirtings (base) boards etc) and furniture as it gives the impression of wood grain.

Dry brushing
Suitable for large walls especially those with various imperfections. Use for an aged paint effect on furniture working in the direction of the wood grain or lengthways.

Faux plaster
Suitable only for a wall finish.

Frottage
Use on any surface with a suitable type of paint.

Granite
Use on surfaces that realistically could be made from this type of stone.

Wrought Iron
Use on surfaces that might realistically be made from iron.

LEFT: Combing is a very versatile effect and looks surprisingly good on floors, especially in bright colours.

Lacquering
Use only on furniture.

Lapis lazuli
Use on small objects that would realistically be made from lapis lazuli.

Leather
Use where leather would realistically be used.

Lining
Use on any surface with the correct type of paint slightly diluted so that it flows easily.

Mahogany
Use where mahogany would realistically be used.

Malachite
Use on small objects that would realistically be made from malachite.

Maple
Use where maple would realistically be used.

Marbling
Use on any surface where marbling would be appropriate, but floating marble must be done on a flat surface.

Oak
Use where oak would realistically be used.

Pewter
Use on objects that might realistically be made from pewter.

Pine
Use where pine would realistically be used.

Ragging
Generally used for walls. Can also be used on furniture with suitable paints.

Roller fidgeting
Use only on walls because of the large flat area needed to achieve the effect. It masks imperfections.

Sky
Ceilings and walls naturally lend themselves to this effect.

Spattering
The easiest way to use this technique is on to a flat surface.

Sponging
Usually used on walls, but can also be effective on furniture.

Steel
Use on surfaces that might realistically be made from steel.

Stippling
Suitable for walls or furniture using water-based or oil-based paint respectively.

Stone blocking
Use on surfaces that realistically could be made from this type of stone.

Tartan (Plaid)
Can be used on any surface as a panel or border of any width or size.

Tortoiseshell
Use on small objects that would realistically be made from tortoiseshell.

Trompe l'oeil panelling
Walls are suitable. Requires

ABOVE: Choose a wide expanse of wall for spattering, as it can get a bit messy!

extensive marking up to make sure all the panels are well proportioned and evenly spaced.

Verdigris
Use on objects that might realistically be made from copper.

Walnut
Use where walnut would realistically be used.

Wood graining
Use where the particular type of wood would realistically be used.

Woodwashing (wood staining)
Use only on bare wood.

TEMPLATES

You can use these templates at this size or scale them up. Enlarge them on a photocopier, or trace the design and draw a grid of evenly spaced squares over your tracing. Draw a larger grid on another piece of paper and copy the outline square by square. Draw over the lines to make sure they are continuous.

PENNSYLVANIAN DUTCH TULIPS

page 192

SANTA FE LIVING ROOM

page 200

GUSTAVIAN LIVING ROOM

page 164

SCANDINAVIAN BEDROOM

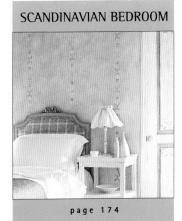

page 174

STENCILLING

page 95

DOOR PANELS

page 172

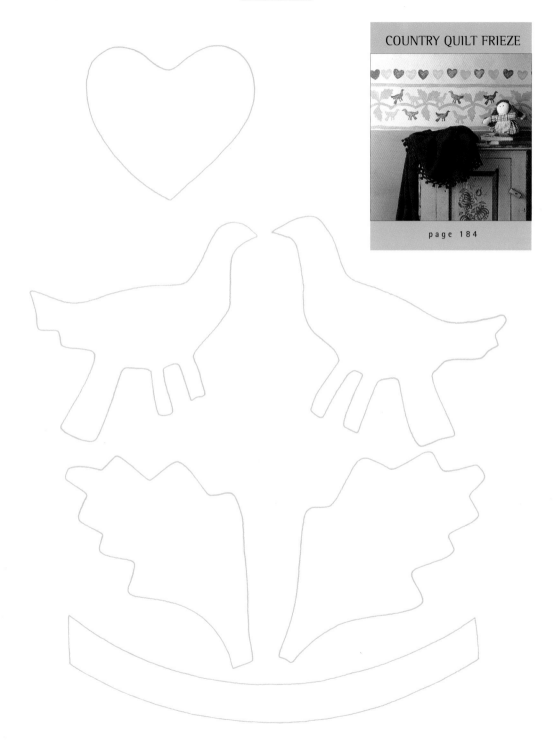

COUNTRY QUILT FRIEZE

page 184

RENAISSANCE HALLWAY

page 168

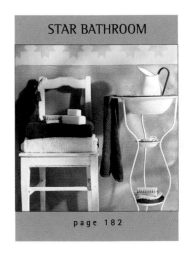

STAR BATHROOM

page 182

MEXICAN HALLWAY

page 196

STAMPING

page 97

INDEX

PICTURE CREDITS

E.T Archive: p 6, 8, 9, 11

ACKNOWLEDGEMENTS

The publishers would like to thank Foxell & James Ltd, 57 Farringdon Road, London, for lending their equipement for photography.

SUPPLIERS

The speciality materials and equipment that you will require for the projects featured in this book are available at any good art-supply shop.

USA

Adventures in Crafts
Yorkville Station
P.O. Box 6058
New York, NY 10128
(212) 410-9793

Art Essentials of New York Ltd
3 Cross Street
Suffern, NY 10901

Createx Colors
14 Ariport Park Road
East Granby, CT 06026
(860) 653-5505

Dick Blick
P.O. Box 1267
Galesburg, IL 61402
(309) 343-6181

Heartland Craft Discounters
Route 6 E., P.O. Box 65
Genesco, IL 61245
(309) 944-6411

Hofcraft
P.O. Box 72
Grand Haven, MI 49417
(800) 828-0359

Sandeen's
1315 White Bear Ave.
St. Paul, MN 55106
(612) 776-7012

Stencil House of New Hampshire
P.O. Box 16109
Hooksett, NH 03106
(603) 625-1716

UNITED KINGDOM

Crown Paints
Crown Decorative Products Ltd
PO Box 37
Crown House
Hollins Road
Darwen Lancashire

Blade Rubber Stamp Company
2 Neal's Yard
London WC2H 9DP
(0171) 379 7391

The Stamp Connection
14 Edith Road
Faversham
Kent ME13 8SD

Brodie and Middleton
68 Drury Lane
London
WC2B 5SP
(0171) 836 3289
Brushes, lacquer, metallic powders, oil and acrylic paints and powder pigments. Mail order.

Green and Stone
259 Kings Road
London SW3 5EL
(0171) 352 0837
Brushes, crackle varnish, linseed oil, scumble glazes, shellac, stencil card. Mail order.

Stuart Stevenson
68 Clerkenwell Road
London EC1M 5QA
Gold and silver leaf and other gilding and art materials. Mail order.

Farrow and Ball
Uddens Estate
Wimbourne
Dorset BH21 7NL
Specialist paint suppliers.

Fired Earth
Twyford Mill
Oxford Road
Adderbury
Oxon OX17 3HP
Specialist paint suppliers.

Grand Illusions
2-4 Crown Road
St Margarets
Twickenham
Middlesex TW1 3EE
Specialist suppliers of paint effects materials.

ICI Dulux
(01753) 550 555 for stockists of paint.

Homebase
(0645) 801 800 for stockists of paint and decorating materials.

Wickes
(0500) 300 328 for stockists of paint and decorating materials.

Do-it-all
(0800) 436 436 for stockists of paint and decorating materials.

NOTES

NOTES

NOTES

NOTES

NOTES

NOTES

NOTES

NOTES

40